The Business Culture in Spain

For Mam and Dad
without whom the journey
would not have been taken.

The Business Culture in Spain

Kevin Bruton

Butterworth-Heinemann Ltd
Linacre House, Jordan Hill, Oxford OX2 8DP

A member of the Reed Elsevier plc group

OXFORD   LONDON   BOSTON
MUNICH   NEW DELHI   SINGAPORE   SYDNEY
TOKYO   TORONTO   WELLINGTON

First published 1994

British Library Cataloguing in Publication Data
Bruton, Kevin
   The Business Culture in Spain
   I. Title
   650.0946

ISBN 0 7506 1831 0

Printed in Great Britain by Clays, St Ives plc

Contents

Series preface

The need for the present series of country books on business cultures arose from the success of Business Cultures in Europe, which was first published in 1990, reprinted 1991, and went into a second edition in 1993. Thereafter, it was felt that the topic of business culture in the major countries in the European Community (EC) was deserving of a larger canvas than that afforded by a mere chapter. Hence a short series of country books is initially contemplated, beginning with Germany and continuing with further publications on Spain, France and the United Kingdom.

All the books in the series have a number of features in common, the most outstanding of which is probably the need to arrive at a tenable definition of 'business culture'.

If a country's 'culture' can be defined as 'the state of intellectual development among a people', then 'business culture' might be held to be 'the state of commercial development in a country'. But the concept of business culture surely embraces this and much more: it also takes in the beliefs, attitudes and values that underpin commercial activities and help to shape the behaviours of companies in a given country. These companies, in their turn, develop their own individual 'corporate cultures', which, put simply, manifest 'the way we do things round here'.

Implicit in the definition of a country's business culture provided above is the fact that there is no such thing as a single, homogeneous European business culture. Europe contains as many business cultures as it does countries. Although the similarities between the business cultures in Europe are legion, so are the differences.

What are the determinants of the business cultures of European countries? What are the factors affecting the similarities and differences between countries? It is self-evident that the relationship between business and government, the shape and orientation of the economy, the financial institutions, and the trade unions all exert a profound effect on the business cultures of all European countries. But is, for example, the attitude of business to green issues equally significant for the business cultures everywhere in Europe? Is, say, the practice of élitism sufficiently wide-spread to count as a determinant of business cultures in all European countries? The answer in both cases is 'no'.

In other words, the business culture in a particular country grows partly out of what could be called the 'current business environment' of that country. Yet business culture is a much broader concept because, alongside the impulses that are derived from the present business environment figure the historical experiences of the business community, such as the periods of hyper-inflation in Germany in 1923 and, in the west of the country, again after the Second World War. In Spain the legacy of Francoism is still a phenomenon the business community is striving to overcome. Of equal significance for the business culture are the future hopes and aspirations not only of business but also of society at large in a given country. How long, for example, should people work in any one week in the 1990s and beyond?

The books in the series focus on the business culture of the country concerned in the late 1970s, throughout the 1980s, and into the mid-1990s. The individual chapters in the books concentrate on those determinants of business culture that are held to be significant for the country under review. Some of the determinants are common to all the countries in the series; others are relevant for only one or two.

The authors of the books in the series have not hesitated to use foreign words and concepts in their works, because such expressions contribute much to the depiction of the nuances in the business culture of any country. They have, however, been at pains to provide a translation of the term in the foreign language on its first appearance in the book.

A conscious attempt has been made to use the common statistical base provided by the Organization for Economic Co-operation and Development (OECD) wherever possible, and especially with regard to major economic indicators such as growth rates and inflation, so that the reader can make meaningful comparisons between countries. Where common statistics are not available, reputable national sources have been used. Sources have been indicated for all figures and tables.

Towards the end of every book in the series a list of publications has been provided in the form of sources and suggestions for further reading. Here only standard works or publications have been included that might stimulate the reader to delve deeper into special aspects of the business culture in the country under review. These lists should not be regarded as exhaustive.

The authors trust that an appreciation of the business cultures in the major EC countries will lead to a better understanding of the structures and strategies of industries, markets and consumer preferences in the countries covered in the series. While it may not constitute the most important element of a practitioner's knowledge, cultural fluency in any one country could make that vital difference between actually gaining a contract or merely coming close.

Collin Randlesome

Preface

Since the mid-1980s, Spain has experienced a boom unprecedented in its history, as the tremendous socio-economic and political changes of the past 30 years have come to fruition under a stable democracy, proud to be a member of the EC. Indeed, Spain led the EC in rapid growth, in the second half of the 1980s, with an average annual GDP growth rate of 4.5 per cent. Rising domestic demand has been accompanied by real increases in incomes, greater employment, and growth in company investment, industrial production and corporate profits. What strikes the foreign observer above all else, however, is the genuine enthusiasm and outward-looking philosophy of Spanish business people and their companies. The introduction of the Single Market was viewed by most Spaniards not just as the real start of fuller integration with Europe but as the opportunity for Spaniards to parade their country's many virtues to the outside world. The Olympic Games in Barcelona, Expo '92 in Seville and the choice of Madrid as cultural capital of Europe in 1992 were obviously important events in themselves, but, more crucially, symbolized the further aspirations of Spaniards to cast off the final shackles of an isolationist past and become important players in the Europe and world of the future.

In the late 1980s and early 1990s, Spanish companies therefore became caught up in an infectious popular enthusiasm for more contact with Europe and the wider world. Optimism and the desire to compete successfully with companies in other countries that have not had to experience Spain's long recent period of political and economic repression coexist with apprehensiveness and anxiety about the consequences of free, unfettered trading. In addition, unemployment rates, which were the highest in the EC, threatened to put a brake on prosperity in the 1990s.

The dynamism of the business culture in Spain is evident in a number of ways, which include:

- Continuing steady, if unspectacular, growth in the Spanish economy following the boom years of 1988 and 1989, with GDP improving during 1985–90 by an average of 4.9 per cent compared with 3.4 per cent

for Germany, 3.2 per cent for France and 3 per cent for the United Kingdom.
- Export success, with manufactured exports rising by 11 per cent in 1991, partly the result of government initiatives to raise Spain's export profile through the chambers of commerce at home and government offices abroad.
- Very high levels of investment in plant and machinery, often through imported technology, in order to modernize industry.
- An explosion of interest among the business and the wider community in the activities of Spanish and international companies, revealed by the plethora of publications emerging in the 1980s – *Comercio e industria* (circulation up from 34,000 in 1983 to 144,000 in 1987), *Actualidad Económica, Dinero, España Económica* (issued in 1989 as a supplement to the prestigious weekly news journal *Cambio 16*), etc.

Spain's business culture also has a number of weaknesses that need to be addressed in the 1990s and beyond. The principal deficiencies are as follows:

- The very high proportion of small companies, often with a conservative mentality and prone to foreign takeover or collapse through free competition.
- Inadequate numbers of suitably trained people, at all levels from shopfloor to management.
- Public services and infrastructure, especially roads, railways, health, education, post and telegraph, which are inferior to those of most of Spain's EC partners and, in some cases, deteriorating.
- The lack (in 1994) of a social compact between government and trade unions, and the threat this causes to economic policy and company planning and profitability.
- Continuing ETA terrorism, which is crippling, economically, the Basque region, the traditional heartland of Spain's heavy industry.

The Spanish government is tackling some of these deficiencies by increasing investment in infrastructure and attempting to overcome the problem of terrorism. The terms of Spain's EC accession in 1986 meant that Spanish business was preparing for 1992 and the completion of the Single Market before most other EC countries. The preparation has often been painful but it has also been painstaking, so that Spain's business culture, despite its weaknesses, is in a better position than ever to play its part in the opportunities opened by a year, 1992, which had so much symbolic importance for Spaniards.

The traditional weaknesses, however, inherent in a large proportion of

Spain's agricultural system, based upon the equally inefficient **latifundios** or large tracts of land in the South and the **minifundios** or tiny plots in the North West, continues to hold back Spanish economic growth and to undermine the efforts of the business community. Spanish agricultural products are moving gradually towards parity of price with other EC countries, and although they enjoyed a competitive price advantage in 1989, this disappeared in 1993. Under the terms of Spain's EC accession, restrictions will continue until the end of 1995 on the export of certain products, including oils, fruit and vegetables, which the Spaniards produce too cheaply for the comfort of the French and Italians.

In November 1988, the European Commission sanctioned a new system of aid to small farmers in Spain that parallels existing schemes in other countries and benefited half a million Spanish farmers to the tune of 20,000 million pesetas yearly up to 1992. The aid, half funded by the EC and half by central government, was intended to put Spanish agriculture on a more competitive basis with its Northern neighbours. New machinery and modernization to reduce the costs of harvesting mostly went to farmers under the age of 35 in an endeavour to rejuvenate the agrarian workforce. The new subsidies, strictly awarded on the investment potential of small farmholdings, supplement youth programmes previously initiated by the government to assist 30,000 young farmers. If the reforms are eventually successful, Spain will become more efficient in its agriculture and the subsidizing of surplus produce by the EC. In addition, the Spanish government produced a Rural Employment Plan in 1992 designed to halt the decline in agricultural employment by allocating 114 billion pesetas to rural areas, with Andalusia receiving 70 per cent of total funds.

Opportunities for foreign investment in Spain have been, and are still, increasing, as the customs barriers and taxes that made it difficult for foreign firms to compete previously have gradually been removed since EC entry in 1986. The Spanish government has actively promoted such investment from abroad, and the different regions have followed suit, encouraging joint ventures or acquisitions of Spanish firms.

A new breed of entrepreneurs is emerging in Spain, as a business career becomes fashionable for many from the wealthy classes. The new business executives will have an MBA from a US university or from one of the flourishing Spanish business schools, which have barely been able to cope with the avalanche of prospective students. Management training is expanding at a phenomenal rate, and the ambitious aim is to turn out 'Euromanagers' able to operate with equal facility in a variety of business environments. Language training, mainly in English, is finally being taken seriously, although it will be decades before Spain produces, if it ever does, sufficient numbers of linguistically competent business people to obviate the need for British companies to have staff who speak Spanish.

Spain's infrastructure and public services have also improved dramatically in recent years, especially since the government's unprecedented 40 per cent increase in public works investment in 1989. Trunk roads and motorways have been expanded. Business communication has been made much easier by the upgrading of domestic airports and a subsequent upsurge in business travel. A high-speed rail link between Madrid and Seville has recently been constructed. This will eventually allow high-speed trains to run from northern Europe to southern Spain and across to the Portuguese capital of Lisbon.

Spanish consumers have seen the arrival of hypermarkets and out-of-town shopping centres and have eagerly bought products from all over the world. At the same time, Spanish designers have forged a worldwide reputation, which in turn has attracted foreign companies to Spain. With over 55 million foreign visitors in 1993, the Spanish tourist industry continues to be a dynamic force in the economy, generating growth, providing employment and stimulating investment and development. Industry is booming, as Spain sets out to be the high-tech capital of southern Europe. British companies have barely begun to discover a country that does not just have tremendous potential in itself but also provides a walkway to the Spanish-speaking countries of Latin America and to the historically linked countries of the Arab world.

The business culture of Spain encompasses many aspects, of a formal and an informal nature, which are discussed in subsequent pages. It is worth highlighting a number of the most important:

- The gradual devolution of power from central to regional government.
- The opening up of the economy, its financial institutions and forms of business enterprise.
- A labour market that still provides labour costs cheaper than most other EC countries but also has inbuilt rigidities.
- A trade-union structure dominated by two unions that have a high public profile, out of all proportion to a low membership base.
- The emergence of a powerful Employers' Confederation of organizations that is growing ever stronger.
- An education and training revolution that is designed to elevate Spain's workforce to the standard in Germany.
- The lack of real interest in the environment and the absence of an environmental industry.
- The growth of an entrepreneurial spirit and the preparedness to express this on an international stage.

Finally, the opportunities for penetrating the Spanish business culture by non-Spanish companies and investors are thoroughly examined in Chapters 12 and 13, which paint the overall background and sketch in the regional dimension of doing business in Spain.

Kevin Bruton

Acknowledgements

I would like to thank Peter Donaghy and Mike Newton for permission to refer to their book *Spain: A Guide to Political and Economic Institutions*.

I wish to extend my thanks also to *El Pais* and *Cambio 16* for permission to use again tables which were first published in *Business Cultures in Europe* (ed. C. Randlesome, 1990). I am similarly grateful to *The Economist*.

My gratitude is also due to the OECD, whose publications are available through Her Majesty's Stationery Office (HMSO), for allowing me to replicate statistics relating to major economic indicators.

On a personal basis, I wish to thank Victor Villar-Hauser and Linda George for providing me with information on the environment in Spain. Lastly, I owe a debt of gratitude to my wife, Ann, and my children, Louise and Nicholas, for their patience, forbearance and support in my writing of this book.

1 Business and government

Introduction

The business world in Spain has had to come to terms with some of the most dramatic changes in the structure of government experienced by any Western European country in the last 30 years. Leaving behind the authoritarian and centralized dictatorship of Franco, which for most of the period between 1939 and 1975 effectively isolated Spain from the rest of Europe, Spanish business has, though not without continuing problems, successfully confronted the challenge of transforming itself, over two decades of fragile democratic governments, into a significant competitor in the Western world. Spain is now an established parliamentary democracy with a constitutional monarch, Juan Carlos I. Parliament comprises two elected chambers, with the Congress as the lower chamber, with supreme legislative power comparable to the House of Commons, and the Senate, as the upper or revising chamber, carrying out similar functions to the House of Lords. The rights of Spaniards individually and collectively are enshrined in Spain's Democratic Constitution of 1978, which also paved the way for a regional government system.

The impetus given by EC membership (1 January 1986) has propelled the Spanish economy – and much of business with it – into the forefront of world economies, with booming growth in the late 1980s outstripping that of most other countries. (Real GDP growth in Spain in 1988, for instance, at nearly 5 per cent was 1.5 percentage points above the EC average.) In 1991 and 1992 there was an inevitable slowdown in economic growth as Spain slid into a recession shared by her EC partners. Spain, nevertheless, in the mid-1990s, is in a much more competitive situation than ever in its history. The problems and successes need to be set within the context of a new framework of democratic central and regional government.

Central government – 1982 to 1993

Spain has experienced a remarkable and peaceful transformation to a healthy and stable democratic government, which has been in the hands of the Socialist Party of Felipe González, Prime Minister since 1982 and victor in three further general elections in 1986, 1989 and 1993, although the 1993 result left his party without an overall majority and precariously propelled into negotiating with minority parties to retain control. The transitional period in modern Spain's emergence from the dark years of Franco ran from 1975, the year of Franco's death, until 1977, when the Union of the Democratic Centre, a centre–right grouping no longer in existence, was in government under the leadership of Adolfo Súarez, King Juan Carlos' nominee as the man who would help him steer Spain towards democracy. The transition could truly be said to be over when Spaniards elected González with an overwhelming majority in October 1982. Since then González has followed a social democratic path of moderation, combining centre–left social policies with centre–right economic and fiscal policies.

The tight monetarist policy pursued by successive socialist governments has been based upon containing inflation, promoting greater freedom and flexibility in business and carrying through a policy of industrial 'reconversion', i.e. a rationalization and modernization of Spain's heavy industry. EC accession in 1986 has assisted the government in its objective of opening Spanish business up to European competition. This 'cold shower' of competition for Spanish industry after years of protection from tariff barriers has met with mixed reaction from the business world. The González government policy in large part though was determined by a number of major economic deficiencies inherited from the Franco era, including:

- The multiplicity of small firms (i.e. employing less than fifty people) in Spain, estimated to constitute some 90 per cent of all companies.
- Technological backwardness *vis-à-vis* established Western democracies.
- The survival of an inefficient agricultural system, largely backward.
- A relatively low level of education and training in the population, with the loss of many skilled workers abroad during the Franco era.
- The Francoist legacy of corporatism, i.e. the large role within the economy occupied by a massive infrastructure of State-owned industries, characterized by bureaucratic overmanning and heavy financial losses.

González's incoming 1982 government also faced a decade of rapidly deteriorating macroeconomic indicators, following the first oil price shock. Spain's performance in this period was substantially worse than other European economies, especially in employment. Spain's unemployment rate in 1982 was 16.2 per cent compared with an EC average of 9.3 per cent, while inflation at 13.8 per cent was also higher than the EC's 9.3 per cent.

Following 1982, the government's implementation of a stabilization programme featuring monetary and budgetary policies that converged on the policies of EC member states, as well as action to moderate wage rises, allowed progress towards reducing inflation, which was moving into single digits by the end of 1986, and towards improving the balance of payments, which, after a decade in the red, finally went into the black in 1984.

Despite a manifesto promise in 1982 to create 800,000 new jobs in Spain, González's first period in office actually saw unemployment increase by almost a million to reach 21 per cent in 1986, the highest in the OECD. The increase was in large part the result of the government's industrial 'reconversion' policy, a major restructuring of Spain's overmanned steel mills and shipyards, which awakened trade-union militancy at the massive job losses entailed.

González won his second general election in June 1986, a victory founded largely upon his success in achieving EC membership for Spain on 1 January that year and upon the absence of an effective opposition party. The government's economic policies continued much as before, but with Spanish industrialists now trying hard to come to terms with the fierce competition from other EC member states.

In the first two years of EC membership, an estimated 150,000 small firms went to the wall as a result of foreign competition, as Spanish business paid the price for moving from a protected economy to a competitive one. Customs barriers and taxes that made it difficult for foreign firms to compete previously have gradually been removed since 1986, allowing a flood of imports into Spain. In fact, in the first year of membership, imports to Spain from the EC went up by 32 per cent while trade between Spain and the EC moved from a surplus position of 268,000 million pesetas in 1985 to a deficit for Spain of 139,000 million pesetas in 1986. In other words, the reduction of tariff barriers in 1985, which reduced Spanish products' average 25 per cent price advantage over competitors to half that level of 12.5 per cent, saw a 400,000 million pesetas boom for EC competitors in 1986. Further tariff cuts, with the last (10 per cent) in 1993, have benefited other EC countries and have seen the demise of many thousands of Spanish companies, especially in vulnerable sectors such as light engineering (including manufacturers of bicycles, motorcycles, electrical appliances and machinery), clothing and some food industries.

The initial reaction of some Spanish business people was to affirm that increased imports from Europe merely provided jobs elsewhere in the EC and that the loss of competitiveness of Spanish firms would be disastrous in the long term for Spanish industry. More enlightened employers, along with the government, reject this view and claim that a significant proportion of the increase in imports has been due to plant and machinery urgently needed to modernize and revitalize industry into more dynamic competitive attitudes. Additionally, the government points to a continuing substantial increase in Spanish exports to the EC over the period 1986–93 as proof of the fact that there are Spanish industries competing successfully in Europe.

While companies like the Valencia-based Tycesa group, which manufactures Western Europe's best-selling Lois jeans, demonstrate that Spanish business can be as efficient as any in the world, there is evidence that many Spanish industries still fear competition. The **Confederación Española de Organizaciones Empresariales** (CEOE) (main employers' confederation), has carried out studies revealing the extent to which the legacy of corporatism persists, and claims that at no point in the government's negotiations for EC entry was there any discussion of the private sector's role in the economy. Instead the question was debated in terms of what the government was or was not doing to help business.

In 1987 and 1988 there was a major turnaround in the Spanish economy, with unemployment starting to move downwards from a high point of over 21 per cent to stand at 15.9 per cent at the start of 1992. The improvement reflected the government's promotion of special employment programmes and tax incentives to industry to create new jobs, as well as a 30 per cent rise in real domestic demand between 1983 and 1989 (compared with an EC average of 18 per cent). The improvement, however, was short-lived as Spain entered the post 'annus mirabilis' year of 1992, with the OECD expecting Spanish unemployment once again to exceed 20 per cent and stand at almost double the rate of Spain's EC partners. Unemployment therefore continued to prove the most intransigent of problems facing González, and almost cost him general election victories in 1989 and 1993.

Fixed investment and investment in plant and machinery continued to rise healthily in the late 1980s (averaging 15 per cent annually) while net capital inflows remained high into 1993 and 1994, revealing direct investment in Spanish business and real estate by foreign companies and increased foreign participation in Spanish firms.

In 1991 and 1992 there was more moderate growth in Spain, partly reflecting policy measures taken in response to the overheating in 1989 and the first half of 1990. After expanding twice as fast as potential output between 1985 and 1990, domestic demand slowed in 1991, led by a decline in car sales and housing starts and a drop in business investment.

Government fiscal policy, in the late 1980s and early 1990s, generated rises in government tax revenues, especially from higher income taxes, and a major campaign was launched to stamp out the widespread tax evasion that has been endemic in Spanish society for decades. Extra tax receipts were used in part to finance additional government expenditure.

Inflation, a major success story for González's government over a 6-year period from 1982, which saw a reduction from 13.8 per cent to 5.2 per cent, started to rise, however, in 1989, and a 1991 year-end figure of 7 per cent only started to fall slowly in 1992 and 1993.

A continuing headache for the González government in the late 1980s and early 1990s lay in continued opposition from the trade-union giants, the socialist **Unión General de Trabajadores**, or UGT, and the communist Workers' Commissions, to which further reference will be made (see page 67). A general strike on 14 December 1988 was the trade-union response to government attempts to force through parliament a Youth Employment Programme to create 800,000 temporary jobs on minimum wage levels. A further half-day strike in May 1992 and a planned general strike in the autumn of 1992 represented protests at government cutbacks in unemployment benefit. Following a one-off expansionist budget in 1989, which aimed to improve Spain's infrastructure and public services, the government reverted to a more cautious approach, with successive budgets more restrictive. Indirect tax increases (with the standard VAT rate rising from 12 per cent to 13 per cent) and higher social security contributions are expected to outweigh a small decrease in income tax and a substantial rise in social spending.

After booming growth from 1987 to 1989, GDP slowed to 2.3 per cent in 1992 and, more disturbingly, to 1 per cent in 1992, with a predicted (by the OECD) fall of 0.6 per cent in 1993. The OECD projection for 1994, however, is a 1.7 per cent rise, which compares with forecast rises of 1.5 per cent for France, 1.4 per cent for Germany and 2.9 per cent for the UK. See Table 1.1.

Central government – the challenge of the mid-1990s

In his fourth general election triumph of 6 June 1993, González's Socialist party won 159 seats in the 350-seat lower house of the Spanish parliament, seventeen seats short of the absolute majority it had held since taking office in 1982. González's investiture as prime minister was supported by two regional parties, Catalonia's Convergència i Unió (Convergence and Union) with seventeen parliamentary seats and the Partido Nacional Vasco (Basque National Party) with five. González's intention was to remain unallied with a minority government but with the possibility of governing in coalition with either or both of the regional parties sometime in the future. González's election victory dashed the hope of the centre–right Partido Popular (Popular Party), which opinion polls had predicted would end the socialists' long period in power, although the Popular

Table 1.1   *Spain's growth rates, 1977–93*

Year	(%)
1977	3.0
1978	1.4
1979	−0.1
1980	1.2
1981	−0.2
1982	1.2
1983	1.8
1984	1.8
1985	2.3
1986	3.3
1987	5.5
1988	5.0
1989	4.8
1990	3.7
1991	2.3
1992	1.0
1993	−0.9

Source: OECD

Party, increasing its total of parliamentary seats from 107 to 141, strengthened its position as an alternative government-in-waiting and, incidentally, as the standard bearer of many, if not all, business interests in Spain.

While González was wrestling with mounting economic problems at home in 1993, he was at least able to present the Spanish electorate with one indisputable 'coup'. The Spanish premier, during the EC Edinburgh summit in December 1992, had successfully negotiated a doubling of the development aid Spain received through the EC 'cohesion policy', in return for Spain's support of the Danish opt-outs from the Maastricht treaty. As a result, EC structural funds will rise by 27.4 bn ECU in 1999 from 18.6 bn ECU in 1992 and a new cohesion fund created by the Maastricht treaty will allocate 2.6 bn ECU to Spain, Portugal, Ireland and Greece. The additional EC funds are intended to assist Spain in meeting EC environmental standards and in upgrading transport networks. Good news on the EC front was very welcome to a González government battered by speculation against the peseta throughout 1993, which forced an 8 per cent devaluation in the spring and further losses with the collapse of the ERM in the summer.

On the domestic front González, following his June 1993 election win, promised Spaniards a further package of austere economic measures in efforts to control a growing budget deficit and to reverse the downward trend of GDP. Already an emergency economic package in July 1992, which included income tax and VAT rises, general expenditure cuts and a new privatization programme, had aroused the opposition of both the trade unions and employers' organizations, which claimed that the measures had not been fully debated. González, following his election victory, acknowledged that a new agreement with the trade unions and employers represented his greatest challenge in the mid-1990s. Such a pact would seem to be the *sine qua non* of future wage moderation and control of inflation.

Since the tripartite agreement between government, employers and trade unions, the Economic and Social Accord, came to an end in 1986, a new consensus has seemed increasingly remote yet still appears crucial if the government is to press ahead with plans to spend more on the infrastructure essential for Spain's businesses to compete successfully. An ambitious programme to raise the share of infrastructure expenditure within GDP to almost 2 per cent per year by the mid-1990s from 0.9 per cent in 1987 (mainly on roads and railways) is accompanied by plans to give priority to education and training in order to overcome hard evidence of a growing mismatch between employer demand and labour supply. Both aims will need to be realized if Spain's economic boom of the late 1980s is to be translated into long-term stable growth and a healthy business culture within which individual Spanish businesses can flourish.

Regional government – the system

The regional government system ratified by Spain's Democratic Constitution of 1978, which laid down the legal basis for the establishment of seventeen regional governments, or **autonomías**, with elected parliaments, represents in Spanish history a totally new framework within which business must operate.

The relation between central and regional government in Spain has been worked out in a succession of 5-year plans, the latest of which relates to the period 1992–6. In broad terms, while central government decides overall policy for taxation and income, social security contributions, defence, foreign affairs, internal security and justice, the seventeen autonomous regions have considerable independent powers. They, however, vary from one region to another. Three types of transfer of central government monies are made to the regions:

- Automatic transfers, decided by size of population, per capita income, area size, degree of isolation, relative poverty, etc. These types of transfer are not subject to negotiations.

- Transfers via an **inter-territorial compensation fund** (FCI), usually for new investments aimed at correcting regional disparities and therefore distributed according to the infrastructural needs of each region.
- Transfers of central government funds for earmarked purposes.

Regions have the right to levy certain taxes, e.g. wealth taxes, and also to add surcharges on government income tax. Operating within the guidelines of the 1987–91 5-year plan, regions were allocated wide discretionary powers over expenditure, although the degree of spending autonomy varied across regions, with only a few, for example, having *full* responsibility for education and health.

The process of negotiating the 1992–6 5-year plan was laborious – twenty-five meetings over 3 months – and contentious, as regions pressed for greater responsibilities while central government sought tighter financial control. The principal innovations in the new 5-year plan are as follows:

- For the first time regional budgets will be co-ordinated very closely with central government budgets, especially with a view to the convergence criteria of the Maastricht treaty.
- A new system of subsidies for education is designed to eliminate previous arbitrary subventions.
- Greater autonomy is given to regions, especially for new investment.
- Major efforts will be made to secure a more fair operation of the inter-territorial compensation fund, which had been heavily criticized by the poorer regions during the previous 5-year plan for actually benefiting the richer regions.

Local authorities, i.e. town and provincial councils, also exist with considerable freedom over expenditure but not over raising of revenue. The regions' and local authorities' expenditure has grown since 1978 and accounts, for instance, for half the spending on state education, a fifth on health care, and two-thirds of total fixed investment. The trend throughout the 1980s was toward greater regional expenditure rather than local decentralization. The combined public deficit of all regions in 1991 was 1.1 per cent of GDP and rising fast. Central government attempts to rein back the regions' expenditure were, however, constantly compromised by the Socialist party's concern to perform well in local elections. The loss of the Socialist party's absolute parliamentary majority after the June 1993 general election meant that Spain's arguably most famous regions, the Basque Country and Catalonia (which includes Barcelona), were given an unprecedented opportunity to seek greater financial autonomy, since the Basque and Catalonia nationalist parties were left holding the balance of power.

These two regions have each had their major problems in recent years. The Basque Country, historically one of the leading industrial areas of Spain, especially for shipbuilding and iron and steel, has been crippled economically by the long ETA terrorist campaign, which has driven many firms to move to safer parts of the country and inhibited foreign investment there. Catalonia, a prosperous area with a powerful regional government, was host of course to the 1992 Olympic Games in Barcelona, which took place, however, against a background of complex and bitter disagreements between central government, regional government and the town council over the infrastructural and service arrangements for the Games.

Thus, the 1993 general election result left the Basque and Catalonia nationalists able to condition support for González in parliament upon greater financial devolution from Madrid. The head of Catalonia's regional government, Jordi Pujol, has consistently sought to reduce taxes paid by Catalonia to Madrid and to gain complete control over the allocation of subsidies in his region. Pujol views the establishment of a 'central' bank for Catalonia as a key element in greater financial independence. The Basque Country has borne the brunt of central government's industrial 'reconversion' programme, which has closed down many old-style heavy industry plants and reduced employment. The Basque nationalists seek greater corporate tax concessions and higher subsidies from Madrid so as to revive industrially depressed areas.

Regional government – the business dimension

Writers on Spain have often claimed that a more accurate name of the country would be 'The Spains', since within its frontiers the differences of landscape, climate, peoples, languages and cultures are probably greater than in any other country in Western Europe. The regions of Spain are, unsurprisingly, therefore resurgent and expansionist, a reaction against the centralized authoritarianism of the Franco era, and a reflection of enthusiasm for being part of a thriving democracy now integrated into Europe. Indeed, financial assistance from the EC has increased dramatically to assist massive investment in infrastructure, and, since 1989, Spain has overtaken Italy as the EC's biggest recipient of regional development funds. The regions have spent heavily to attract inward investment and increasingly businesses need to recognize this devolutionary dimension. As people in Spain have become disenchanted with central government, regional parties have gained strength and now rule three regions (the Basque Country, Catalonia and Galicia) as well as holding 32 seats out of 350 in the national parliament. Virulent forms of regionalism, as in the case of the Basque terrorist group ETA, have been on the wane, however, as the vast majority of the population demonstrate their rejection of violence and extremism (ETA's political wing, Herri Batasuna, lost two of its four remaining parliamentary seats at the 1993 general election).

Madrid, although an important industrial region, has never enjoyed the automatic supremacy over the rest of Spain as, for instance, Paris over France or London over the UK. The region of Catalonia, based around Barcelona, has traditionally led the way in industrial and commercial endeavour, and has vied both with Madrid and with the heartland of Spanish heavy industry in the Basque Country. Other regions have sprung to prominence in recent years, notably the Valencia area, Asturias in the north (and especially the Gijón–Oviedo–Avilés triangle) and Andalusia in the south (with Seville as its capital). Mass tourism has boosted many regions, including of course the Canaries and the Balearics. The end result is a regional framework that encourages new initiatives, such as regional universities and science parks, and actively welcomes and supports inward business investment.

The regions' ability to do this stems from an explosion in their public expenditure during the 1980s, as additional resources have been decentralized from central government. According to the Bank of Spain, public expenditure in the regions rose from 1.8 per cent of total public expenditure in 1981 to 16 per cent in 1990, and from 0.9 per cent of GDP in 1981 to 9.4 per cent in 1990. The bulk of this expenditure derives from central government transfers, since the regions only raise 1 per cent of their own revenue and have inevitably encountered charges of wasting money. Demonstrably, the big three regions of Madrid, Catalonia and the Basque Country have benefited most from central grants, while some of the smaller regions, such as Extremadura and Castile–La Mancha, remain rooted in agricultural deprivation. Table 1.2 provides some idea of the economic importance of the different regions in relation to their size and their level of development.

Spain is of course a major agricultural as well as industrial nation. A rapid review of the traditional regional strengths in agriculture and industry provides an essential background for understanding the regional dimension of the business culture in Spain.

Spain's main crop is the olive, mostly grown in Andalusia, with 40 per cent of the world total coming from Spain. In wine production, Spain rates third in the world league after France and Italy. Wheat is the most common cereal and, with maize and rice, is grown in the north and along the Valencian coast. Fruit is Spain's main agricultural export, with oranges and lemons grown in Valencia and Murcia, and bananas in the Canaries. Cotton and tobacco support the economy in Andalusia, while potatoes and vegetables sustain the Galician economy. Asturias is the prime dairy farming region of Spain. Despite export success, Spain still imports

Table 1.2 *Spain – the regional picture (1987)*

Region	% All GDP	% Total population	Index of level of development (national average = 100)
Catalonia	19.5	15.4	108.7
Madrid	16.5	12.5	115.5
Andalusia	12.5	18.1	95.6
Valencia	10.4	9.8	105.8
Basque Country	6.0	5.5	103.9
Castile–Leon	5.9	6.6	92.0
Galicia	5.8	7.4	80.8
Canaries	3.7	3.9	100.3
Aragon	3.5	3.0	97.9
Castile–La Mancha	3.3	4.3	89.2
Balearics	2.7	2.8	110.3
Asturias	2.7	2.8	90.9
Murcia	2.2	2.7	98.7
Extremadura	1.8	2.8	79.0
Navarre	1.5	1.3	101.1
Cantabria	1.3	1.4	92.5
La Rioja	0.7	0.7	99.4

Sources: *Banesto* and *Economist*

agricultural produce. The fishing industry is the fifth largest in the world in tonnage of catch, with over half of this accounted for by the Basque Country and Galicia. Very little fish is exported, and indeed Spain is a net importer of fish and seafood. In the first 2 years of EC membership, Britain's export of agricultural produce to Spain increased 1,000 per cent, with seafood exports improving 1,500 per cent.

In industry, Spain's traditional strengths have been in heavy industry. In shipbuilding Spain is sixth in the world league, with El Ferrol in Galicia, Cadiz in Andalusia and Cartagena in Murcia the leading centres. Spain's mineral resources have long been a pillar of the economy. Asturias is renowned for coal and mercury; Andalusia for lead, uranium and copper (particularly the Rio Tinto mines near Huelva, built by British engineers in the last century); and Catalonia for potash. These industries supply the iron and steel industries around Bilbao in the Basque Country, and also in Catalonia and Asturias, which in turn supply the motor, aircraft and shipbuilding industries. Textile factories (cotton, silk and wool) have been a mainstay of the Catalonian economy since the eighteenth century. The Valencia region is responsible for major export markets in the footwear industry.

In general terms, most of the regions have invested in infrastructure and are modernizing capital equipment and production processes while attempting to support new high-tech industries and the improved banking and financial institutions that underpin all such endeavours. It is already true to say that a foreign business or business person interested in investing in a particular region must deal direct with that region and not just with Madrid. Increasingly the trend will be for all significant business and financial decisions to be made in the appropriate region. The final chapter of the book will highlight more recent regional developments and business opportunities.

Conclusion

In the 1993 general election, the Left (the Socialist Party plus the alliance of the ex-Communists, Izquierda Unida or United Left), polled 11 million votes, while the Right obtained 8 million votes – 3 million more than in 1989. The Nationalists – Catalans, Basques, etc. – had 2.5 million votes. According to Fernando Schwartz, columnist of Spain's leading newspaper *El País*, writing in the *European* following the election:

> . . . in the end, what counts is that this election signalled the end of an era. Irrespective of the winner, the electors have chosen to indicate three things: that they are fed up with the old Socialist steamroller, that they still believe in the Socialists' progressive policies and that, maybe, they are beginning to think of trusting the Right once more.

Certainly González, in addressing the nation in the early hours of 7 June 1993, when his re-election as prime minister was confirmed, promised that central government would heed the message given by the voters. For the trade unions this implied giving priority to measures to bring down the unemployment figures. The leaders of Spain's business community interpreted González's statement as meaning further measures to introduce flexibility into the labour market and facilitate business expansion. The regional parties, holding the balance of power, perceived immediate opportunities to increase the powers of regional government at the expense of the centre. Few commentators were in any doubt that the election heralded a redrawing of the map of governmental responsibilities between Madrid and the seventeen regional parliaments.

2 Business and the economy

Introduction

It is difficult to overstate the tremendous structural changes in the economy with which Spanish business has had to contend in the past 30 years. An industrial revolution that in other European countries happened over 100 years before only really arrived in Spain in the 1960s, a decade that witnessed an acceleration of the exodus from countryside to town, the phenomenal growth of mass tourism, and the first stages of an opening up of the economy to the Western world that was to culminate in Spain's EC accession in 1986. Throughout this entire period, the massive state-owned industries continued to dominate the Spanish economic scene, even, it could be argued, in the mid-1990s, when the principal challenge for much of Spanish business is to throw off the shackles of recent decades by major capital investment in plant and machinery in order to be able to compete successfully in the modern era against established Western rivals. Thus the advent of a marketing-oriented philosophy has come later to Spanish companies, but the performance of many of these companies, e.g. in the new sectors of electronics and telecommunications, shows that the new lessons are being applied.

With consumer demand growing at 7 per cent in 1989, Spanish firms enjoyed fuller order books, and company profits mounted in the late 1980s. These profits, helped by a fall in oil prices, led to unprecedented levels of investment in Spain and the creation of new jobs. With the economy growing at 5 per cent in 1988 and 1989 however, the difference between what Spain produces and consumes was imported, and, as a result, foreign firms in the late 1980s benefited enormously. The response of Spanish firms was dynamic, however, with government estimating that in 1987 and 1988 at least 40 per cent of industrial capacity was updated. Even though growth levels in the early 1990s slowed down to half the previous level, Spanish economists remained optimistic that growth would rise again once all the results of capital investment are seen.

In the early 1990s, companies in all sectors faced difficult times as Spain, along with her major EC partners, battled with recession and the challenges presented by planned EC economic convergence. The González government consistently reiterated its commitment to the Maastricht line on convergence, although of the five targets set by Maastricht – inflation, interest rates, budget deficit, government debt levels and exchange rate stability – Spain currently meets only one, government debt. The government announced its own 'convergence plan' for the 1992–6 period, with the main aims and objectives as follows:

- GDP growth to average 3.5 per cent p.a.
- Creation of 1 million jobs.
- Investment growth to average 3.5 per cent p.a.
- Inflation to fall to 3 per cent by 1996.
- Public deficit to fall to 1 per cent GDP by 1996.

Inconsistencies in the plan were immediately apparent, such as the projected growth rate being inconsistent with falling inflation and job creation. Spanish employers, though, were boosted by measures in the plan that would reduce labour market rigidities.

As Spain moved into post-1992 depression, however, with GDP falling by 0.9 per cent and unemployment rising by 22.7 per cent in 1993, the government's 1993/4 budget was uncompromisingly tough. Its main features were:

- Widespread expenditure cuts e.g. housing 0.4 per cent, defence 1.5 per cent, industrial and energy policy 4 per cent and transport subsidies 7.5 per cent.
- Rises in social security contributions, with employers paying 0.4 per cent more and employees 0.1 per cent.
- Tax increases on tobacco and alcohol of 5 per cent and 10 per cent respectively.
- A pay freeze for civil servants, along with a freeze on public sector recruitment.

There were, however, a number of encouraging aspects to emerge from the budget, as infrastructure investment was to remain at 5 per cent of GDP, in line with the convergence plan, while it was announced that Spain in 1993 was a net recipient from the EC to the tune of 204 billion pesetas, a 20 per cent rise on 1992.

Heavy industry and INI

Long dominated by the state-owned industries of the public holding company, the **Instituto Nacional de Industria (INI)** (National Institute for Industry), the sheer economic power of heavy industry has set the business agenda in prominent regions of Spain such as the Basque Country.

The government's 'industrial reconversion' policy, launched in 1984, aimed to enhance competitiveness by adjustments to capacity and cuts in the workforce, financial restructuring and technological modernization, supported by public subsidies and credits. By the end of 1987, 85 per cent of envisaged job cuts (approximately 71,000) in shipbuilding, carbon-based steel, specialist steels, etc., had been achieved.

The restructuring was initially successful. INI in 1988 registered its first profits since 1975, after record losses in 1983. Thirty firms went and, of the fifty-eight firms still left in INI, forty-nine improved their financial position by the late 1980s, with the largest profits being made by Endesa, the electricity giant, and Inespal, aluminium manufacturers. Government aid bolstered INI's success in the late 1980s but this was no longer possible, according to EC directives, after 1992. By the 1990s, however, famous INI firms such as Iberia, the Spanish airline, and Ensidesa, the steel company, were in trouble again, and the government decided to reorganize INI so as to make state firms more competitive and attract private sector finance.

INI was one of the fifty biggest trading groups in the world, and in Spain accounted for more than 30 per cent of all production in a wide range of industries – coal, iron and steel, shipyards, electricity, aluminium, air and rail transport, etc. INI's industrial production is 10 per cent of industrial GDP and its internationalization process has gone further than most Spanish firms, with over 30 per cent of its sales (1988) coming via exports as against the average for all Spain of 14 per cent. Its R & D budget was again 23 per cent of the national total, and INI employed 140,000 people.

INI's consolidated losses in 1992, though, were 58 billion pesetas, a marginal improvement on the 85.7 billion losses of 1991, but a performance poor enough to harden the government's resolve to restructure it. As a result, from 31 December 1992, INI was split into two, to form a new private sector holding company, Teneo, which comprises more than half the old INI subsidiaries. The forty-seven firms within Teneo represent 80 per cent of INI's turnover, 56 per cent of the total workforce, and 70 per cent of exporting capacity. Teneo firms must survive without government subsidy and compete with private sector companies in the single European market. Teneo includes Iberia and Inisel (Spain's leading defence electronics manufacturer, which is merging with private sector competitor Ceselsa). Teneo was designed to be profitable from the outset and may at some future point seek flotation.

The government's overt privatization policy is to be extended, with the establishment of another new holding company to which will be

Table 2.1   *Spanish tourism*

Year	Numbers of foreign tourists (millions)	Income (millions $)
1975	30.1	3.404
1980	38.0	6.967
1985	43.2	8.151
1986	47.4	12.058
1987	50.5	14.760
1988	54.2	16.686
1989	54.1	16.174
1990	52.0	18.593
1991	53.5	19.004
1992	55.3	21.035

Source: *Anuario El País*

transferred some of INI's top firms. This new grouping will not be launched on the stock market but stakes in individual firms will be sold off and the state will lose full control in some cases. INI will then be left with the largest loss-making companies, in mostly heavy industry, such as mining, shipbuilding and steel-making, which still has a workforce of 50,000. As central government squeezes public expenditure, prospects for these traditional firms appear bleak.

Tourist industry

It is estimated that 1 million Spanish families work directly or indirectly in the tourist trade, which thus constitutes the largest employer in Spain, providing work for roughly 10 per cent of the active population. Spectacular growth since the 1960s shows little sign of plateauing out, despite problems, as new tourist sectors continue to spring up and diversification of supply attracts more tourists to the cultural hinterland or away from the high season.

What is astonishing about Spain's revenue from tourism (Table 2.1) is that it is generated by very low levels of expenditure, as revealed by comparative figures for 1986, which show that Spain's income of 12.058 million dollars was matched by only 1.512 million dollars of expenditure, an income/expenditure ratio of 8 to 1. France, the United Kingdom, the United States, and countries such as Switzerland and Austria had virtual parity of income/expenditure in the same year, while former West Germany's ratio was 1 to 3.

Despite a continuing upward graph in foreign tourist numbers, Spain experienced a few 'blips' in the early 1990s as 'sun and sand' holidays began to be less expensive in other European countries, notably Greece, Portugal and Turkey. For a country where tourism accounts for more than twice the share of GDP generated by the car or steel industry, this was a problem the Spanish Tourist Board could scarcely afford to ignore. With a budget of 25 million dollars in 1992, the Tourist Board set out to attract higher-spending, professional people to Spain, running thirty different colour press advertisements and five TV commercials in the national and international media all over Europe, Asia and the Pacific. The aim was to build upon the high international profile enjoyed by Spain in 1992 due to Expo '92 in Seville and the Barcelona Olympic Games. Assisted by devaluation of the peseta, foreign tourist numbers increased in the first half of 1993 by 3 per cent over the same period in 1992, and further rises in the second half of 1993 and in 1994 were expected to give a renewed boost to the tourist industry.

Construction

The construction industry in Spain, after experiencing severe crises between 1975 and 1985, is now more powerful than ever, with a workforce of 1 million and some of the top companies in Spain, notably Cubiertos and Dragados. The industry contributed a weighty 9 per cent of GDP in 1990, the fifth successive year of significant growth. Companies benefited in the late 1980s from a property boom, especially in Madrid and Barcelona, and from increased government spending on infrastructure, particularly roads, and on public works generally. Housing, leisure and tourist facilities are still being expanded rapidly across the country, not just in the construction boom towns of Seville, Barcelona and Madrid.

While Seville witnessed the construction of the Expo '92 pavilion buildings and major infrastructural works, including the high-speed rail link with Madrid, Barcelona was even busier. An estimated 430,000 m^2 of new office space was completed in the 2-year period up to mid-1993, one third of which is outside the city centre. The Olympic Village, built in the city's old industrial area by the waterfront, included a new hotel and more than 100,000 m^2 of offices by developer G Ware Travelstead. On the Avenida Diagonal, one of Barcelona's most famous up-market streets, Swiss insurance company Winterthur has built 48,000 m^2 of offices in a development which includes a hotel, shops, apartments and parking for 2,300 cars. While opportunities for new development inside Barcelona's core area are restricted, several new business parks have been taking shape on the outskirts. The largest is local developer Dorn's Augusta Business Park, which, at 500,000 m^2, also lays claim to being southern

Table 2.2   *Major companies in the construction industry (1988)*

Company	Sales (billion pesetas)	Employment
Dragados	156.0	11,692
Fosca	101.2	13,300
Cubiertos	97.1	6,843
Entrecanales	95.0	7,500
Ferrovial	86.2	3,660
Hasa-Huarte	73.0	4,406
Agromán	69.4	5,623

Source: *Anuario El País*

Europe's biggest. At San Cugat, where a new road tunnel was opened in 1991, UK developer Higgs and Hill is busy with a project that will offer 20,000 m² of space in four buildings, set in landscaped grounds.

Madrid has been equally frenetic. Following an office and housing construction boom between 1987 and 1990, an estimated 200,000 m² of top quality new space was completed in the central business district in 1991, with a further 54,000 m² and 71,000 m² scheduled for 1992 and 1993 respectively.

Some of Spain's leading banks have large holdings in the top companies, e.g. Banco Central Hispanoamericano in Dragados and Banesto in Agromán. In addition, the tourist boom and the vast urban expansion of the 1960s and 1970s saw the emergence of many medium-sized companies and thousands of small companies (often in the black economy). Despite economic crises in the late 1970s and early 1980s, the more recent construction boom has seen new companies springing up in the industry.

The complex ownership structure of many Spanish construction companies, especially large ones, made it difficult in the past for foreign companies to penetrate the market. However, the late 1980s and early 1990s finally brought significant foreign penetration. Major holdings in Agromán and other Spanish companies have been taken by the German construction giant Philipp Holzmann. The French company Bouygues also has considerable holdings, as does Heron International.

The British company Butler Building Systems Ltd is currently undertaking the expansion of the Coca-Cola plant in Madrid as a result of a joint venture with a Spanish company. The British firm reports successful co-operation with its Spanish partner, founded upon the local firm's knowledge of the domestic market, a liberal attitude by the Spanish authorities to innovative design and the absence of any protectionism.

Large multinational hotel groups began to enter the Spanish market in a major way in the late 1980s. Holiday Inn opened its first hotel in Spain (Madrid) in 1985. It has since invested in the construction of hotels in Seville, Barcelona and in ten other large towns, offering low-priced, functional accommodation in direct competition with more traditional accommodation. In 1990, Trusthouse Forte concluded a joint venture agreement with the oil company REPSOL to develop 100 Little Chefs and Travelodges in Spain, while the French hotel groups Accor and Air France were planning to create hotel chains in Spain through franchising arrangements.

Inevitably, the construction sector was not immune to the economic slowdown in 1992, a year in which 103,000 jobs were lost in the industry and turnover dropped 6 per cent on 1991. The major problems of the industry are the excessively high number of very small companies – of 65,000 construction firms in Spain, it is estimated that 90 per cent employ fewer than ten people – and over-dependence on state-financed public works, with central and regional governments accounting for one third of all construction across the country. The latter problem is a double-edged sword, however, since the industry is banking on further massive state investment in infrastructural developments. The Ministry of Transport and Public Works planned to spend 1 billion pesetas on infrastructure in 1993, 65 per cent of which was destined for road-building. And in the spring of 1993, central government approved a plan for the development of infrastructure (Plan de Desarrollo de Infraestructuras) which would invest 18 billion pesetas in the next 15 years.

The new technologies

Expo '92 in Seville was more than just an exhibition. Spain, and particularly the southern region of Andalusia, hoped to use Expo '92 as an infrastructural springboard to create a high-tech 'supersite' known as Cartuja '93. Universal expositions are meant to reflect the latest technological advances and cultural trends, and act as a stimulus for change in the future. In the same way that the last Universal Exposition in Osaka in 1970 marked Japan's emergence as a power to be reckoned with, Expo '92 was intended to mark Spain's 'coming of age' as an advanced democratic nation.

At the end of Expo in October 1992, after attracting 20 million visitors and vast sums of money, Expo officials had achieved a great public relations success. Their main aim in staging the coveted world fair, however, was to attract long-term investment to southern Spain and raise Andalusia's profile in the European business arena. Buildings and roads are being re-used in what will rank as Spain's first World Trade

Centre and a showpiece scientific and technological research complex. Hosting six research centres, the complex, or *Centro Superior de Investigaciones Científicas* (CESIC), combines public and private investment and is designed to draw a string of international names to Seville. Cartuja '93, as the project is called, has already won contracts from multinationals such as IBM, Siemens, Phillips and Rank Xerox. Others are expected to follow suit. The end result will be a remarkable marriage of the old with the new; Cartuja Island, only 7 years ago an arid wasteland surrounding an ancient Carthusian monastery from which Columbus set off to discover America, is destined to become the symbol of a new high-tech age of discovery.

Whereas firms engaged in the new technologies have been shedding staff throughout the world at the start of the 1990s, in Spain the rapid expansion continues. The number of firms in this sector has increased from virtually nil at the start of the 1980s to fifty-eight in 1987 and over 100 in 1992, with further rises in companies and employment projected, just as other countries in Europe experience contraction.

The Spanish high-tech boom is deliberate government policy, embodied in the National Electronics and Information Technology Plan, which, over an initial 3-year period ending in December 1993, allocated a budget of 158,000 million pesetas to the sector, 45 per cent from public funds, 38 per cent from the Centre for Technological and Industrial Development and 17 per cent from the EC. The prime aim of the plan, which provides continuity with previous plans, is to give priority to advanced technologies that improve the competitiveness of the production system and the efficiency of infrastructure and services. The Plan is subdivided into seven main areas:

1 Electronics and data processing.
2 Advanced automation.
3 Stimulation of research in the pharmaceutical industry.
4 Development of biotechnologies, and chemicals and materials technology.
5 Support for basic industries and transformers.
6 Technological infrastructure.
7 Industrial and technological modernization in firms.

The telecommunications industry has also grown rapidly, supported by a national telecommunications plan for 1989–92, which envisaged continuing government investment in the industry of the level of 500,000 million pesetas annually, equivalent to between 1.1 per cent and 1.5 per cent of GDP. Spain's first communications satellite, Hispasat, was placed in orbit in 1992, one of its first major tasks being to support transmission of the Olympic Games in Barcelona.

The high-tech sector has always seen Spanish firms linked with foreign multinationals, following the pattern of the 1986 agreement between the Spanish telecommunications company Telefónica and ATT, which led to the construction outside Madrid of Western Europe's biggest microchip factory. There has been little indigenous development, and increasing foreign investment has been promoted by the government. Foreign multinationals now completely dominate production in Spain, especially in electronics and information technology. Consumption of personal computers and software is largely through import. Even Telefónica, one of Spain's biggest companies, has lost its telecommunications monopoly (except for the basic telephone service) and foreign participation in the company increased from 3 per cent in 1982 to almost 30 per cent in 1992.

The major foreign multinationals in Spain include Alcatel-Standard Eléctrica (a subsidiary of the Compagnie Générale d'Electricité de France), ATT Network Systems and LM Ericsson-Intelsa. Another Scandinavian firm, Electrolux, bought two firms in Catalonia in 1988, while a number of electronics industry giants have plants in Spain, e.g. IBM, Olivetti and Rank Xerox, mostly in the Madrid and Barcelona regions (although Fujitsu and Siemens also have plants in Malaga). The government favours European networks or joint ventures in this sector. An example is Spain's flight simulation company, CASA, which is engaged in an initiative to develop high-speed computers with other EC companies that form part of a pan-European consortium linking industry and research institutes, supported by the EC ESPRIT programme.

In terms of domestic retail consumption, Spain has recently experienced rapid growth, and demand remains very strong. For example, the home computer market expanded nearly ten-fold between 1986 and 1989, from a total value of 204 million pesetas to 1,900 million pesetas. In addition, the sales value of personal computers rose from a total of 33.5 billion pesetas in 1986 to 37 billion pesetas in 1989. Both markets are set to continue growing as Spanish consumers catch up with their EC neighbours. The scope for penetration by foreign companies is equally great.

Spain also has plans for developing a series of science and technology parks. The first of these, Malaga Science Park, is a showpiece designed to make the maximum impact worldwide. The Malaga area is a logical choice for the first major initiative designed to attract European investment, with 100,000 foreigners legally resident in the Malaga area. The 415-acre science park cost 4.2 billion pesetas, and Hughes Microelectronics (part of General Motors) has committed itself to an 8 million pesetas investment in the park.

Malaga is selling itself as southern Europe's high-tech boom town. With Spain's fifth largest metropolitan area and third largest airport, Malaga claims to be Europe's fastest growing city below the Madrid–Rome axis. The city's university has recently opened a Computer Science and Telecommunications Faculty, which will assist in the training of the 2,500 high-tech personnel, mostly local people, who will be working in the park by the year 2000. Inducements to foreign companies to set up bases in the area are considerable, with subsidies and incentives offered to cover 100 per cent of all running expenses and up to 50 per cent of a company's investment. In addition, Malaga is an area designated by the EC and the regional government of Andalusia as a priority development zone.

Despite the frantic activity in Spain during 1992, Malaga is in no hurry to fill the park but is determined to find the right occupants in specified fields, i.e. telecommunications, microelectronics, industrial and office automation, IT, lasers, new materials, renewable energies and biotechnology. Though the city suffers from poor land communications, the completion of the dual-carriageway link to the new Seville–Granada motorway will assist industry.

Car industry

Spain is the fourth-largest car manufacturer in the EC, a long way behind Germany and France but not far short of Italy and ahead of the United Kingdom. Cars account for a quarter of all Spain's exports, and the industry employs nearly one in ten of the working population. All Spain's car producers are now foreign-owned and have been pouring investment into the industry to the tune of 150 billion pesetas a year; VW–Seat maintains a design centre employing 800 people. In terms of exports Spain leads the field in Europe, with almost 1.3 of 1.8 million cars manufactured in 1992 destined for the export market.

Spain also has great potential for continued growth, with labour costs, although rising in the 1990s, still lower than in Germany and France, with a workforce surplus and the possibility of further modernization to reduce costs. Thus Ford and General Motors locate their small models in Spain while Renault divides production between Spain and France. The Japanese company Suzuki is also planning to work with VW–Seat to produce a new small car in Spain. Ford also plans to manufacture two new cars at its Valencia plant. The smaller model alone, destined for launch in June 1996, will mean an additional production of 400,000 cars a year.

While 1992 was a good year for the car industry with record levels of production and export (see Table 2.3), 1993 saw the industry suffering the first effects of recession. While a small fall in sales was widely predicted, figures for the first half of the year pointed to a year end fall of 20 per cent over 1992. Despite these 'hiccups', the Spanish car industry looks set for further long-term growth, especially in a domestic

Table 2.3 *Spanish car production and exports (1992)*

Company	Production No. of cars	%	Exports No. of cars	%
Seat-Audi-VW Group	551,380	30.7	452,224	35.4
General Motors	366,416	20.5	321,652	25.3
Ford	310,753	17.4	200,594	15.7
Fasa-Renault	309,538	17.3	182,278	14.3
PSA Group	252,528	14.1	117,622	9.3
Total	1,790,615	100	1,274,370	100

Source: Anuario El País

environment where car ownership is low at 300 cars per 1,000 inhabitants, the equivalent of the EC 25 years ago and 20 per cent lower than the EC average.

PYMES

The proliferation in Spain of small and medium-sized firms, which are known as **Pequeñas y Medianas Empresas (PYMES)**, has determined major shifts in business planning in the last few years. Coinciding with Spain's presidency of the EC in the first half of 1989, the Industry and Energy Ministry launched a new programme geared to 1992 specifically for PYMES. Its triple aims were the promotion of R & D; the strengthening of greater communication at European level, with the involvement of PYMES in such schemes as SPRINT, BC-NET, EUROPARTENARIAT, etc.; and the streamlining and simplification of often bureaucratic management structures.

In the late 1980s and early 1990s also, a movement towards new (for Spain) types of financial corporations, holding companies and consortia, was becoming evident, as the PYMES, supported by the government, sought wider markets in Europe. Thus Spanish firms, both large and small, began to diversify horizontally, i.e. into areas unconnected with the business of the original firms, and vertically, i.e. in the same sector. Cement and real-estate firms are the leaders in this diversification drive, which has attracted state-owned concerns. Indeed, the state tobacco company, Tabacalera, has pioneered the trend, since it now owns twenty-six firms unconnected with tobacco, and they account for 25 per cent of all sales, a figure which rose to 50 per cent in 1993.

Table 2.4 *Spain's exports (1977 and 1991)*

	1977 (%)	1991 (%)
France	16	20
Germany	11	16
United Kingdom	6	8
Italy	5	11
Other EC	11	16
North America	11	5
South America	10	3
Other	30	21

Source: OECD

Exports, imports and foreign investment

In terms of exports, Spain's performance over the period 1960–87, an annual improvement of 8.5 per cent, was the highest in the OECD with the exception of Japan, Greece and Turkey, and comfortably outstripped the EC average at 5.8 per cent, Germany at 5.7 per cent, the United Kingdom at 4.2 per cent and France at 6.4 per cent. Imports, however, in the same 1960–1987 period, were the highest in the OECD at 10.4 per cent, which compares with the EC at 5.8 per cent, Germany at 5.9 per cent, the United Kingdom at 4 per cent and France at 6.5 per cent.

The major trend in exports saw trade with the EC commanding a larger share during the 1980s, while exports to North and South America, perhaps surprisingly, fell from 21 per cent of overall exports in 1977 to 8 per cent in 1991 (Table 2.4). Within the EC, Spanish companies were most successful in the 1980s in increasing exports to the United Kingdom, Italy and France.

Despite the fact that government economic policy since 1982 has actively welcomed increased foreign investment in Spanish companies, in the early 1990s, there was widespread fear in Spain that the process of foreign takeovers was going too far. With Spain's rapid growth, opportunities mushroomed for foreign investors and multinationals, especially in the private sector, where long isolation had left few Spanish firms in a position to withstand competition. State-owned industry and the banks have, to date, been most successful in defending Spanish interests.

Spain's chemical, cement and insurance industries have been the most popular sectors for foreign investors, with, for instance, the Kuwaiti group

KIO buying Enfersa, a chemical group, previously part of INI, under a cloud of scandal and corruption. In sectors where foreign competition accounts for one-third of total consumption, and where Spain's biggest company, Ecros, is only in twentieth place in Europe, it is difficult to resist foreign intervention. Thus it was no surprise in July 1992 when North America's largest cement producer, Cementos Mexicanos (CEMEX), acquired Spain's two largest cement companies, Valenciana de Cementos and Sanson.

Arab and British companies have been at the forefront of recent wholesale acquisitions of Spanish firms. While the Arabs have bought into food companies, stationery, finance and real estate, British companies have led the field with, for example, the acquisition of Alhambra Publishing by the Pearson Group, the olive oil giant José Guiu by Unilever, and the Petromed refinery by BP.

Most purchases, though, have been worth less than 50 million pesetas, perhaps suggesting that foreign companies have been buying into Spain gradually, with one eye on post-1992 Europe. The Spanish government has not been averse to selling off state-owned firms to foreigners. Additionally, foreigners spent approximately 300,000 million pesetas a year in the late 1980s purchasing property in Spain.

As was pointed out in the previous chapter (see pp. 7–12) regional inequalities, which have always existed, have become exacerbated in recent years as Spain's growth has generally benefited already prosperous areas, notably the area around the two major cities of Madrid and Barcelona, the Valencia region and the Balearics and Canaries, at the cost of the traditionally poorer agricultural areas of Extremadura, Castile, Andalusia and Galicia. The Basque provinces, the heartland of Spain's heavy industry throughout this century, are in crisis due to the industrial reconversion programme, which has decimated its steel mills and shipyards. Despite specific employment programmes and the establishment of **Zones for Urgent Reindustrialization (ZURs)** in areas hit particularly hard by job losses, there seems little evidence as yet that the nettle of unequal regional development has been grasped by government or the business community.

The Socialist government also inherited sudden wage rises which followed Franco's death in 1975 and which saw real labour costs rise more rapidly in Spain until 1983, admittedly from a very low level, than in any other Western European economy. The rise occurred when real labour costs were actually falling in countries like Denmark and the Netherlands.

While Spanish wage levels are generally lower today than her EC partners, this advantage is to some extent offset by lower productivity levels. As a result, with wage costs still continuing to rise faster than production, the maintenance of high levels of employment constitutes an ever-present challenge.

Although, as was indicated previously, global foreign investment in Spain is growing yearly, there is a major question mark as to whether it is growing quickly enough in a country where indigenous sources of capital are limited and the banks historically (though the trend is changing) have preferred to invest in real estate rather than in industry.

One drawback of the multinational presence is that it does little to stimulate local research. And it is in this area that the structural weakness of Spanish industry is glaringly apparent. According to the OECD, the only member countries to spend less on R & D than Spain are Portugal, Greece and Turkey. Without basic research it may be that Spain's commercial future will remain mostly in intermediate industries such as car manufacturing.

Transport infrastructure

In 1992, Spain introduced its new high-speed train, the Alta Velocidad Española or AVE. The new train will not only revolutionize rail travel in Spain but in an important sense symbolizes a desire to raise Spain's transport and communications system to the level of other European countries.

Spanish geographical realities have always hindered industrial development. Spain stands at a higher average altitude above sea level, 650 metres, than any other country in Europe except Switzerland. Madrid, focal point of road and rail networks, has the highest altitude of any capital city in the EC and, surrounded by mountains, has never been easily accessible from any part of the Peninsula. Communications and transport have been underdeveloped for a number of reasons: the many mountain ranges that have made road and rail construction difficult; extremes of climate in some parts of the country, which may close roads in winter and ruin surfaces; seasonal rivers; the *rías* or fjords in the northwest, etc. In other European countries, such as the UK, the improvement in transport systems in the last century was due to the needs of the Industrial Revolution. In Spain there was no Industrial Revolution until the 1960s, so when the economy and industry picked up to get on terms with other European competitors, the transport system could not cater adequately for the needs of business. In addition, government was slow to respond to obvious infrastructural deficiencies, and after the first oil shock, investment in transport actually declined in real terms.

However, since 1982 and the advent of the first González government, the trend has been reversed. A 1980 plan to extend the motorway network in Spain by 7,000 kilometres in 10 years had only achieved half its objective by 1990. As a result, the government launched a major programme to build 1,700 extra kilometres of motorway and a further 1,200 kilometres of trunk roads by the end of 1992.

One major transport success in the 1980s was the development of domestic air travel, in line with the recommendations of another 1980 plan to strengthen regional airports and facilitate commercial travel. Thus an initial 57,000 million pesetas' investment for the period 1981–6 improved facilities at the airports of Madrid, Barcelona, Seville, Valencia, Malaga, Tenerife, Palma de Mallorca and Santiago. Five other airports important to the tourist trade – Alicante, Ibiza, Lanzarote, Las Palmas and Menorca – also received infrastructural subsidies. The resulting improvements and consequent increase in domestic air travel have been of enormous benefit to the Spanish business community, faced with lengthy alternative journeys by road or rail.

The Spanish national railway network, *Red Nacional de Ferrocarriles Españoles* (**RENFE**), under state ownership since 1941, has received significant government investment in the past decade. Recent improvements include the laying of more double track in mountainous terrain, a central computerized ticket booking system, more electrification and the introduction of better, faster trains. Since 1988, railway investment has risen at a yearly rate equivalent to 1 per cent of GDP. The major part of this expenditure has gone on the introduction of high-speed trains, the AVE, on the Madrid–Seville and Madrid–Barcelona routes, as well as the commencement of an operation, which will go well into the next century, to narrow the gauge to that of Spain's EC partners. Spain's wider gauge of 1.668 metres compares with 1.435 metres in France, and the discrepancy has always hindered freight transport.

The high-speed line from Madrid to Seville is the first stage of a new international rail network, with two connections planned to France and one to Portugal by the year 2000. The Spanish aim is to link into a high-speed European rail network that is currently mapped out only on paper but has a number of significant pieces slotting into place. There is the successful example of the French high-speed train, the TGV; the 2-hour, 427–kilometre Paris–Lyon service alone carries 13,000 passengers a day, 90 per cent of the market. The Channel Tunnel link, opening in 1994, will mean a 3-hour journey from London to Paris and 2 hours forty minutes from London to Brussels. The UK business community may soon be witnessing a passenger or freight journey from the UK to Spain that could be equated with current journey times from London to the outer reaches of Britain.

The AVE Madrid–Seville service, opened in April 1992, has become a symbol of the Spanish desire to project themselves as a rich, progressive European nation. Constructed in great haste and at a cost that could rise to 500,000 million pesetas, six times the original budget, the AVE route has attracted great controversy, with environmentalists speaking of an 'ecological tragedy'. Despite such criticisms, twenty-four high-speed trains have been commissioned from the French company Alsthon, a new railway station has been built in Seville, and Madrid Atocha station has had fifteen new platforms constructed to take the train. Journey times are within the timescale of $3\frac{1}{2}$ hours, which is calculated to be the maximum time that business travellers are prepared to sit on a train.

The regional government which wanted the link to France to be built first, accepted the argument that the route south of Madrid was a priority to ensure the connection of both halves of the country, but exacted a promise from central government of an immediate start on the Madrid–Barcelona–French border AVE. The Basque Country is also pressing for an extension of the high-speed track, but this is not expected until 2002. The AVE will have a dramatic impact on communities hitherto considered distant from Madrid. Ciudad Real, at 200 kilometres, is widely expected to become a dormitory town of Madrid. Apart from expanding the commuter network, the extremely competitive fare prices (tickets ranged from 6,000 to 16,500 pesetas when advertised in early 1992) are bound to appeal to the business and wider community.

The real cost of the AVE project is unknown, and, although many European governments, including Britain's, have been pouring money into their rail networks in recent years, the cost of putting a Europe-wide high-speed rail network in place is extremely high. (The Paris-based Community of European Railways estimates at least £85 billion, at 1985 prices, between now and 2015). Spain, after centuries of isolation, is at the forefront of political and governmental pressure within the EC to transform the vision of a high-speed rail network from southern Europe to Scandinavia into reality.

Conclusion

The Spanish business community faces in the mid-1990s a crisis engendered by the twin requirements of overcoming recession and competing successfully in Europe. In 1992, the index of industrial production fell by 1.7 per cent compared to 1991. All areas were similarly affected, with consumer goods production lower by 1.4 per cent, capital goods by 1.9 per cent, and intermediate goods by 1.7 per cent. A drop in profits accompanied employment losses and company bankcruptcies. Most industrial sectors were hit by a fall in demand and an increase in competition. In 1993, these negative trends continued, with car sales noticeably declining.

Spanish industry is now completely immersed in the European economic scene and confronts the macroeconomic exigencies of the Maastricht Treaty in a free competitive European market. Residual problems, however, create restraints for Spanish industry, most notably the excessive number of small companies, heavy technological dependence upon foreign firms and investment, and a limited international presence. The crisis, nevertheless, is also having a positive impact on Spanish businesses. Companies are finding themselves forced to enact a series of measures in order to survive competitively in Europe. These measures include reducing costs, rationalizing employment, and eliminating bureaucratic structures and procedures. In short, more efficient business organizations are being created, and they will be in a better position to grow and develop once the crisis is over.

3 Business and the law

Introduction

Article 39 of Spain's 1978 democratic constitution recognizes and guarantees the rights of private enterprise in Spain. However, most legislation affecting forms of business enterprise dated back to the 1950s. Thus, the laws governing the legal status of limited liability companies were more than twenty-five years old and obviously in need of reform. In addition, 1950s' legislation related to a business environment in which Spain was pursuing an economic policy of autarky, or economic self-sufficiency, carried out by an authoritarian regime that wanted as little as possible to do with the world outside Spain. The democratic governments of the post-Franco period therefore needed to pay special attention to the legal framework regulating business activities if Spain was to take advantage of EC membership and the revolutionary opening up of markets this entailed. The laws relating to employment, for example, have been extremely rigid and have made it very difficult for businesses to dismiss employees, although the government has promoted flexibility in recent years. In addition, major changes in company law will gradually take effect through the 1990s, as a result of harmonization with EC legislation.

Spaniards have been noted throughout history for a healthy disrespect for authority, or for a feeling that laws passed by the state can either be flouted or used to one's own private ends. Widespread tax evasion has been endemic in Spain for decades, and businesses are not immune from colluding with the banks in dreaming up ingenious schemes to escape paying taxes. Similarly, the Spanish tradition of **enchufe**, an almost untranslatable term which means 'maximizing connections, whether family and friends and whether above or below board, to make progress', is deeply ingrained. The absence of guilt makes Spaniards self-confident and great fun to be around. However, the Spanish have a deep sense of personal pride, or **honor**, and an ill-considered personal insult may have disastrous results on one's business.

The administration of justice

The Spanish legal system is based on the constitution of 6 December 1978. Article 1 of the Constitution proclaims that Spain is a 'social and democratic state based on the rule of law' and that 'national sovereignty resides in the people from whom all powers derive'. The constitution also paved the way for a complete restructuring of the state to allow for decentralization, so that regional parliaments, executives and judiciaries share responsibilities with their counterparts in Madrid.

The longest section of the constitution deals with fundamental rights and the obligation of the state to uphold and guarantee these rights, except in the most exceptional circumstances. Article 10 declares that such rights shall conform to those listed in the Universal Declaration of Human Rights. Three types of rights can be identified: basic human or civil rights, political rights, and socio-economic rights. The last-named category includes, in Article 37, the right to collective bargaining, and ensures the binding nature of collective agreements between management and labour.

Legislation in Spain is of four main types, in descending order of importance: laws, royal decree laws, royal decrees and ministerial orders. The laws are promulgated by the national parliament (the Cortes) and the parliaments of the regional governments, and are invalid or void if they conflict with the constitution.

The Spanish courts are administered by one judge (**juzgados**) or by several judges (**tribunales**) and have different levels of responsibility. The court system is divided into specialist courts that deal with civil, criminal, labour or administrative issues. Appeals may be made to the competent tribunals and, finally, to the Supreme Court (**Tribunal Supremo**). Further appeals can be made to the Constitutional Court (**Tribunal Constitucional**), but only in cases of conflict of the law with the constitution and acts against individual constitutional rights. At regional level, a new tier of judicial authority has been created alongside the new tier of legislative and executive power. Thus each region now has a high court to which disputes over regional law can be referred. The regional high courts, however, all fall within the ultimate authority of the Supreme Court in Madrid.

Finally, legislation in 1981 created the post of the ombudsman (**defensor del pueblo**). His or her role, as legally defined, is to watch over the activities of ministers, administrative authorities, civil servants and persons working for any branch of public administration. All public authorities are obliged to assist him or her in his or her investigations, giving preference over other claimants on their time.

Legal background to business enterprise

Although operating openly in a democratic environment, business enterprises in Spain are still largely bound by a legal framework established during a Franco era in which the business community was 'given its head'. Most existing legislation governing business practice goes back to before 1975, and in the case of the legal status of limited liability companies dates from the early 1950s. The most glaring anomaly is the failure under Franco to compel firms to carry out independent audits, and the consequence has been wide popular mistrust of published accounts. Only in recent years have the majority of firms been persuaded that external auditing is in their own interests, as they learn to take seriously the views of shareholders and employees.

Spain's democratic constitution of 1978 recognizes the rights of private enterprise and states that these should be exercised in accordance with the requirements of the economy and within the general framework of government economic policy. All types of business, except sole trader, are obliged to register their existence in the Mercantile Register of the provincial capital in which the company's head office is located. Thereafter, a record of the main details is kept in the Directorate General for Registration in Madrid. The basic information that must be entered includes name, address, nature of business, date of foundation and capital. Subsequent changes in any of these particulars must be recorded. Foreign companies wishing to establish branches in Spain are required to follow the same procedure, and they must also produce a certificate from their local Spanish consul verifying that they have met the legal requirements of the country of origin. The register is available for public inspection, and the corollary of this is that failure to register a particular aspect could lead to a charge of fraud. Any member of the public may obtain details of specific companies by personal enquiry to the register. The reference number relevant to a company's entry in the register is usually included on the company's official stationery.

Forms of business enterprise

The principal types of company permitted by law are briefly summarized below. A more comprehensive account can be found in Donaghy and Newton's *Spain: A Guide to Political and Economic Institutions*.

Sociedad anónima – SA (company)

This is the most prestigious type of company in Spain, similar in all major respects to a UK public limited corporation (plc) or limited liability company. It can be in the public as well as the private sector, and may be a larger company quoted on the stock exchange or a smaller family business. No minimum size is stipulated but, hitherto, in accordance with 1951 legislation, any company with capital in excess of 50 million pesetas must register as an SA company. New legislation, however, has reduced the minimum capital requirement to 10 million pesetas.

Sociedad de responsabilidad limitada – SRL/SL (company)

This type of company is similar in many ways to an SA but is limited to fifty stockholders and has a minimum capital requirement of 500,000 pesetas. There is no maximum capital requirement. An SL does not have shares, and the capital is divided among the shareholders. This type of company has no minimum capital requirement and therefore offers more flexibility than the SA. They are often found in the retail and service sector, and if an SRL company is quoted on the stock exchange, there are legal restrictions on the transfer of shares. There are, however, few other formal legal requirements on this type of company, e.g. to provide audits or reliable financial information.

Sociedades colectivas (partnerships)

Partnerships are not widely found in Spain, although two types exist in law: the **sociedad colectiva**, or general partnership, with unlimited liability; and the **sociedad en comandita/sociedad comanditaria**, or limited partnership, with a minimum of one general unlimited partner and one limited partner.

Cooperativas (co-operatives)

The most famous Spanish co-operative, Mondragón, in the Basque region, has attracted worldwide attention since its foundation in 1956 and still welcomes foreign delegations of interested politicians, economists and business people anxious to discover the secret of perhaps the world's most successful co-operative. Over 100 enterprises, employing almost 20,000 people (and spanning consumer goods, capital goods, agriculture and construction), constitute a co-operative whose international fame undoubtedly derives from its unique supporting organizations: its own bank, with 100 branches in the Basque region; social security system; medical and hospital care; and a technical college.

The Spanish Constitution encourages the development of co-operatives and a separate co-operative register exists. The Ministry of Agriculture has pioneered the establishment of co-operatives in recent years, in an attempt to overcome the **minifundio** problem of tiny plots of farming land (see also pp. xiv–xv). Both small co-operatives, comprising six or seven plots of land, and very large co-operatives, comprising up to 200 plots, have enjoyed considerable success.

Comerciante (sole trader)

Extremely numerous in Spain, **comerciantes**, or sole traders, are found in many sectors, especially food and drink, retail, and crafts and services. They are automatically members of the local chamber of commerce. Any individual may, subject to regulations, establish his own business with unlimited liability.

Joint ventures

The multiplicity of small firms in Spain has encouraged the government to provide financial incentives to firms to establish joint ventures. Such ventures the government sees as crucial to improving Spain's export performance. There are four main types of joint venture permissible under Spanish law, and all of them enjoy excellent tax benefits.

1   Sociedad de empresa
This is a joint venture corporation of at least three participants, which may themselves be SAs, SLs or individuals, and constitute a separate legal entity. Venturers may contribute capital in cash and/or other assets, but their holding in the joint venture corporation is limited to 30 per cent of their own paid-up capital. The object of this corporation is normally the expansion or modernization of manufacturing facilities, sales promotion, or the requisition of machinery or other assets for exploitation.

2   Agrupación de empresa
This is a grouping of firms that agree, without creating a separate legal entity, to combine to progress the common business interests of their members.

3   Unión temporal de empresa
This is a business agreement, concluded for a fixed or indeterminate time, for the purpose of carrying out a construction, service or supply contract.

4   Cesión de unidades de obra
This provides for an arrangement whereby a subcontract can be passed in part or in full to third parties.

Foreign investment

Usually up to 50 per cent of the share capital of a Spanish company can be bought by foreign investors without prior authorization. Any shareholding in excess of 50 per cent can only be approved by the **Dirección General de Transacciones Exteriores** (Directorate General of Foreign Transactions) where the share capital does not exceed 25 million pesetas. In some sectors, however, the investment percentage requiring authorization is lower, e.g. in shipping, mining, and banking.

Foreign companies therefore have considerable freedom to buy into Spanish companies, the only exceptions being the defence industry and the mass media, where no foreign investment is allowed. Foreign banks are finding restrictions on their operations being removed, while foreign companies are able to set up **sucursales** (branches) in Spain. A sucursal is not, however, a legal entity in Spain, as SAs or SLs are. A branch must also be registered at the Mercantile Register, along with duly notarized documents.

Labour legislation

In 1979, a Mediation, Arbitration and Conciliation Institute (IMAC) was set up as an autonomous administrative body under the auspices of the Ministry of Labour. IMAC's role was primarily to provide conciliation services aimed at individual workers seeking information on their rights before having recourse to the labour courts. Within each province there is at least one labour court, which handles most ordinary cases of dismissals, breaches of contract and social security problems. More serious matters and appeals are sent to the central labour tribunal in the first instance, and at the highest level to the social division of the Supreme Court. However, the existence of IMAC as an independent body was short-lived. Many of its functions were transferred to regional governments, and, in April 1985, its remaining functions and personnel were transferred to the newly created Subdirectorate General for Mediation, Arbitration and Conciliation of the Ministry of Labour and Social Security.

Conclusion

Spain is in the early stages of developing a legal framework within which business enterprise can flourish in a modern European democracy. Much has been achieved in the last 20 years as two difficult and in some ways contradictory challenges were undertaken: the challenge to 'tighten up' and modernize the laws governing the operation of business, and the challenge to open up Spanish business culture to foreign investment and competition. As other chapters indicate, it appears that the challenges are being successfully met, although rigidities remain, especially in employment regulations, which may inhibit further progress. Central government in Spain is fully aware of the need for more legislation in this area.

4 Business and finance

Introduction

The banking system enjoyed a large role under Franco in a country where industry was able to find few alternative sources of finance, although for most of the period up until the early 1970s, the banks found themselves hidebound by a bureaucratic system of rules and regulations, which prevented new initiatives and rapprochement with the rest of Western Europe. Legislation in the 1970s, though, finally relaxed the restrictions to allow new Spanish banks to emerge and also, in 1978, to permit foreign banks to set up in Spain.

The **Banco de España** (Bank of Spain) is Spain's central bank, responsible for supervising the country's banking and monetary system. In this role it performs similar functions to central banks in other EC countries. Private banks have multiplied to approximately 140 since 1985, although half of these are regional or local rather than national in character. They are small by world standards but have been extremely profitable in recent years. There was, however, a squeeze on margins in 1990 and 1991 as the Spanish boom calmed down. Traditionally, the banks have not been internationally minded, but this has changed rapidly since 1986, with alliances being forged with foreign banks as expansion has taken place into foreign markets, and with diversification into a broader range of financial services, leading, for instance, to the establishment of investment banking divisions. The main strengths of Spanish banks have been their strong capital and healthy reserves, while their principal weakness is high labour costs through an overcapacity in branches, estimated by some to be as high as 30 per cent.

Alongside the private banks are the **cajas de ahorros** (savings banks), which may be privately or publicly owned but are run as non-profit-making foundations, somewhat similar to the building societies in the UK. The cajas have become more efficient and competitive in recent years as Spain's financial markets have opened up. At the same time Spain's stockmarkets have begun a late but necessary drive to integrate into EC and world trading.

Although in fields such as pension funds and the insurance market Spain has taken significant strides forward in the past 10 years, this sector still remains some way behind EC competitors and presents considerable opportunity for foreign investment.

The Banco de España

Spain's Central Bank, the Banco de España, was nominally in private hands until 1962, when it was nationalized. In the 1970s, the Banco de España was accorded an important role in managing monetary policy, and is now responsible for the monetary system and for supervising the banking system to the government Ministry of Economy and Finance. In this role it performs similar functions to central banks in other countries.

The Banco de España played a crucial interventionist part in the banking crisis that hit the country between 1978 and 1983, and which affected fifty-one of the then 110 banks operating in Spain. The reasons for the crisis were multifarious, including the oil shocks, the rise in inflation caused by post-Francoist wage settlements, and the tight monetary policy pursued by the first governments of the democratic transition.

The Banco de España was instrumental in establishing a deposit guarantee fund in 1977 to alleviate the crisis for troubled banks or depositors, and itself guaranteed half the fund, to be matched by compulsory deposits from the Spanish banks. The fund, run by its own board of management, was in fact used to provide help for twenty-six banks in financial crisis between 1978 and 1983, as well as to give some protection and/or compensation to depositors.

As the Banco de España's role has moved closer to that of its EC financial counterparts, so inevitably its role has been crucial in supporting real growth in Spain and in determining interest rates. Above all, the Banco de España has endeavoured to carry through the González government's objective of bringing the rate of inflation into line with that of major trading partners, notably countries participating in the European Monetary System, which Spain itself joined on 19 June 1989, with the peseta located, like the Italian lira, within a 6 per cent margin of fluctuation. The Banco de España's success in assisting the downward trend of inflation from the very high levels experienced up to the mid-1980s can be gauged from Table 4.1.

International comparisons reveal that inflation in Spain has been high through much of this period. As pointed out by the 1988–9 OECD *Economic Survey:*

Starting with a small positive inflation differential at the beginning of the 1970s, the margin relative to the OECD average widened dramatically

Table 4.1 *Spanish inflation rate, 1977–93*

Year	(%)
1977	24.5
1978	19.8
1979	15.7
1980	15.5
1981	14.6
1982	14.4
1983	12.2
1984	11.3
1985	8.8
1986	8.8
1987	5.3
1988	4.8
1989	6.9
1990	6.7
1991	5.9
1992	5.9
1993	4.9

Source: OECD

between the two oil shocks, peaking at almost 16 per cent in 1977. It then diminished equally fast to reach a low of 2.6 per cent in 1980 before attaining a new high of close to 7 per cent in 1983. Since then there has been a rather steady narrowing of the gap to no more than 1 per cent in 1988, only temporarily interrupted in 1986 by the introduction of VAT which pushed the level of consumer prices up by an estimated two percentage points.

Inflation started to rise again, however, in 1989, finishing the year at almost 7 per cent. With unit labour costs in manufacturing also rising, the Spanish government in the early 1990s was concerned that inflation would disrupt the strength and confidence generated by recent growth. However, further deregulation and trade liberalization have assisted the Banco de España in keeping inflation to manageable proportions. The government plans to reduce inflation to 1 per cent of GDP by 1996 from 4 per cent in 1991.

In 1992, underlying inflation rose further, partly because of the build-up of demand pressures associated with the Barcelona Olympics and Expo '92. This was mainly reflected in service sector inflation, which in recent years has been the fastest growing component in the Consumer Price Index. In the spring of 1993, a number of changes were made in the way the CPI is calculated, with the objective of making it less volatile and more representative of underlying inflation. The main changes were a higher weighting for services and a lower weighting for food (in line with practice elsewhere in the OECD), a rationalization of the way housing costs were included in the index, and a change in the base year to 1990. On balance, the net effect of the changes was expected to be broadly neutral.

Throughout 1992 and 1993, Spain's Economy Minister, Carlos Solchaga, and Bank of Spain Governor, Mariano Rubis, consistently reiterated that the reduction of inflation was Spain's main priority. As a result the Bank of Spain kept Spanish interest rates high, with the bank's key intervention rate of 12.4 per cent higher than most EC member states. While most commentators in 1992 agreed that the peseta was overstrong within the Exchange Rate Mechanism of the European Monetary System, few were prepared for three currency devaluations within a 9-month period as speculators hit the ERM on 'Black Thursday', in September 1992, forcing an 8 per cent peseta devaluation, which was supplemented by further devaluations of 5 per cent and 8 per cent by May 1993.

An interesting footnote is that, according to IMF figures, Spain is fifth in the world league table of countries in terms of foreign currency reserves. The Banco de España's reserves are higher than those of the United Kingdom, France, Canada or Switzerland. Clearly this is a reflection of international prestige and confidence of foreign investors, and another indication of how Spain has become fashionable in international business.

Argentaria (Corporación Bancaria de España)

In 1991, the central government brought together a number of state-owned banks – the Banco Hipotecario, the Banco de Crédito Industrial, the Banco de Crédito Agrícola, and the Banco de Crédito Local – and other financial institutions to form Argentaria (Corporación Bancaria de España). This creation of a state 'megabank' was greeted with alarm by Spain's private banks. Argentaria represents an attempt by government to establish a Spanish bank of European dimensions. In other EC countries the state banks have had greater weight than in Spain (state banking represents only 13 per cent of the system in Spain, compared with 30 per cent in Germany). The private banks' concern was that Argentaria would monopolize finance for the state sector in a country where 40 per cent of GDP is controlled by the government.

Already by 1993, Argentaria was Spain's number one bank for institutional banking, for mortgage and long-term financing, and for government bond trading and trade finance. Argentaria increased its operating income by 24.6 per cent and pre-tax profits by 25.5 per cent, and the group's cost/income ratio fell from 55 per cent to 53 per cent. In April 1993, Argentaria stated that it would proceed with a 22 per cent share offering, valued at up to $940 million, despite growing political and economic uncertainties.

Private banks

According to a 1985 study, there were ninety-eight banks in Spain – thirty-seven of national scale, thirteen at regional level, and forty-eight at local level. This classification into national, regional or local banks, is preserved by the **Consejo Superior Bancario** (National Banking Council), which operates as a clearing house for information and statistics on the banks and provides a forum for meetings between representatives of the private and public sector banks.

Since 1985, the number of banks in Spain has increased to approximately 140, an increase due to the high profitability of banks since the mid-1980s.

. The trade unions have complained to the government about the excessive profits generated by the banks under a Socialist government, and the government itself is unhappy. In fact, in 1988, the government stepped in to demand that the banks allocate a proportion of their profits to the modernization and restructuring of their operations. The banks themselves were not unwilling, since they have been sensitive to the charges of excessive profiteering.

Banks' profits must be seen, though, in the context of profit generated by companies. A survey undertaken by the Banco de España in 1987 of 4,000 firms revealed a doubling of profits over 1986, and hence the view of a leading banker in Spain is hardly surprising when he asserts: 'When companies do well, we do well. If firms are doubling profits, then no one should be amazed if we increase ours by 40 per cent!' The top ten private banks are listed in Table 4.2.

There was a squeeze on profit margins in 1990 and 1991 as the Spanish boom calmed down, and 1992 saw further falls in a year described by Emilio Ybarra, chairman of Banco Bilbao–Vizcaya (BBV) as 'the worst of the past decade', after seeing his own bank's 20 per cent fall in net profit. Ybarra was expecting a revival in 1993 but his views were not necessarily shared by other leading bankers. BBV's two biggest rivals, Banco Central Hispanoamericano (BCH) and Banesto, also registered considerable slumps in profits in 1992, of 17 per cent and 27 per cent respectively. The Big Three banks, which have massive stakes in Spanish industry, were feeling the effects of bad debts owed to them by industrial companies in which they held shareholdings.

Table 4.2   *Top ten Spanish private banks (1992)*

Bank	Assets (million pesetas)	% Total
Banco Central Hispanoamericano (BCH)	4,782,860	15.91
Banco Bilbao–Vizcaya (BBV)	4,237,852	14.10
Banesto	3,149,245	10.48
Banco de Santander	2,511,548	8.35
Banco Exterior de España	1,542,149	5.13
Caja Postal	1,197,230	3.98
Banco Popular Español	1,128,172	3.75
Banco Sabadell	840,251	2.80
Hipotecario de España	748,770	2.49
Bankinter	679,355	2.26

Source: *Anuario El País*

Table 4.3   *Profitability of Spanish banks*

Bank	Net profit (billion pesetas)		
	1992	1991	% Change
Banco Central Hispanoamericano	60.0	76.5	−17.0
Banco Bilbao–Vizcaya	81.1	101.2	−19.9
Banesto	45.7	62.6	−27.1
Banco Santander	66.2	59.2	+11.8
Banco Exterior de España	21.0	18.9	+11.3
Banco Popular Español	54.5	49.7	+9.6

Source: *The European*

Spain's first two private banks, BCH and BBV, are both the result of mergermania as central government continues to press for link-ups between banks by offering practical inducements, e.g. a 99 per cent exemption on capital gains tax payable after a revaluation of assets. The biggest merger to date, in 1991, created Spain's biggest private bank, the Banco Central Hispanoamericano (BCH). BCH's profile typifies the leading role Spain's top banks play in supporting domestic industry. BCH has extensive industrial holdings, whose turnover accounts for 4 per cent of Spain's GDP. The holdings are in strategically important industries such as petrochemicals, construction and food. BCH owns a 9.4 per cent stake in Dragados, Spain's second largest construction company; an 11.5 per cent stake in Cepsa, the second largest petrochemical firm; and a 19 per cent holding in Campofrío, a major national food group. BCH also holds 26.7 per cent of Spain's biggest property company, Vallahermoso. BCH's main rival, BBV, also has important holdings in three of Spain's principal electrical companies; it owns a variety of firms in the food industry, including Kas and the Savin wine group; is the biggest client of INI, the state holding company; and in recent years, like BCH, has been buying firms in strategically vital areas of industry. Banesto, under the leadership of the charismatic Mario Conde, made rapid progress in the 1980s, but its future was under a cloud, when, following heavy selling of Banesto shares, the Banco de España took over its management in December 1993.

The main strengths of Spanish banks have been their strong capital and healthy reserves, while their principal weakness has been high labour costs. Considerable progress has been made in recent years in overcoming the other main failing, i.e. low levels of internationalization. Despite government pressure for greater concentration through mergers Spanish banks continue to open new branches in an attempt perhaps to dissuade foreign penetration. Spain has approximately three times as many branches as Germany and twice as many as France.

Foreign banks and foreign penetration

The Spanish banks' extensive network of branches is, paradoxically, the reason why foreign banks have been buying up and into Spain. The domestic banks are basically strong, have made large investments in new technology but are still not internationally oriented. Restrictions on foreign banks in Spain have been gradually lifted since the mid-1980s to permit forty banks to operate (twenty from the EC), while ten Spanish banks are foreign controlled. The top six Spanish banks control approximately 75 per cent of the market, and exert continuing pressure on the government and the Banco de España to protect them from foreign competition. Foreign banks account for 16 per cent of total loans in Spain but crucially account for 84 per cent of loans to firms who invoice more than 5,000 million pesetas a year. Unsurprisingly, the foreign banks have complained of being unfairly discriminated against in a context where their highest share of the banking market was 10.6 per cent in 1984, stabilizing since at 9 per cent. It appears also that foreign banks did not benefit as much from the consumer boom in the late 1980s as domestic banks, although 1988 was a particularly good year for them, with pre-tax profits rising by 54 per cent of over 1987.

A number of foreign banks had already acquired Spanish banks in the early 1980s when the Spanish banking system was in crisis. Citibank and

Barclays bought into Spain at that time, and the Deutsche Bank also took complete control of the ailing Banco Comercial Transatlántico in 1989.

The story of Barclays is an interesting one. Beginning with the purchase of thirty-three outlets from the Banco de Valladolid, Barclays then pursued a strategy of opening hundreds of small branches, with a maximum of five staff, across the country, on the basis that more Spaniards are now preferring a 'boutique' approach to the traditional Spanish 'department store' approach in banking. Barclays also made headway in the profitable retail market by offering interest on a range of current accounts well ahead of their Spanish rivals. However, the launch in 1990 by the Banco de Santander, Spain's most aggressive and internationally oriented bank, of the 'supercuentas', or interest-bearing current accounts, which was quickly copied by other banks, has led to a highly competitive situation.

The Banco Santander is linked with the Royal Bank of Scotland in a fascinating compact that allows both banks to expend their international interests. The Royal Bank and Santander came into contact when each was looking for an equal partner with which to expand in Europe. They knew they had no competing activities in each other's markets and soon discovered they were of similar size and outlook. The result, a highly informal partnership, leading to closer ties as the two sides got to know each other, is a strategy that could be adopted by all sorts of companies that want a European network without exposure to risks. The scope of the agreement between the Royal Bank and Santander includes co-operation in Britain and Spain, linking up their computerized fund transfer network, joint ventures in other European territories and pooling information outside Europe. Their retail networks stay separate. The basis of their third country joint ventures was a couple of virtually inactive banks Santander owned in Belgium and Germany, CC Bank Belge and CC Bank. Royal Bank has taken stakes in them, and the partnership has bought into operations in Portugal and Gibraltar.

The opening of Banco NatWest's new headquarters in Madrid in 1991 represented a further stage in NatWest's penetration of the Spanish market. National Westminster Bank is a 99.4 per cent shareholder in Banco NatWest España, and this sizeable interest provides banking facilities in over 200 branches throughout the Spanish mainland. Banco NatWest has over 120 of these, with the subsidiary organization, Banco de Asturias, accounting for the remainder. The network is focused on Spain's major industrial and financial cities: Madrid, Barcelona, Valencia, Zaragoza, Bilbao and Seville. However, the bank is also well represented on the Costa del Sol and the Costa Brava, and has a growing presence in Alicante, Santander and the regions of Asturias and Galicia.

Banco NatWest España is primarily geared to providing a service to the retail, small and medium-sized business sectors of the market.

In addition, it supplies a comprehensive facility for personal account holders through its wide branch network. It also has in-depth experience of mortgage finance and Spanish property purchase procedures, which can often be complicated.

While the experiences of Barclays, the Royal Bank of Scotland and the National Westminster Bank reveal the extent to which Spanish banking has opened up to foreign penetration, there are also numerous examples of the Spanish banks actively seeking foreign investment and alliances. In 1993, the US bank JP Morgan more than doubled its capital investment in Spain's third private bank, Banesto, to 130 billion pesetas, a 5 per cent stake. Rumours of a takeover circulated but Banesto appeared content to attract foreign investment in difficult times, especially with longer-term plans to float Banesto on the New York Stock Exchange.

Other Spanish banks have sought wider-ranging alliances with foreign groups. The Banco Popular Español, Spain's seventh biggest bank, has allied itself with a number of foreign banks in order to develop new services for an increasingly competitive retail market, and although Spanish shareholders now have 54 per cent of Popular's capital, foreign shareholding in the bank, at 46 per cent, is one of the highest in Spain. Undoubtedly, further liberalization of the regulations to allow freer and fairer competition is certain to see foreign banks making further inroads into Spain in the mid- and late-1990s.

Cajas de ahorros (savings banks)

The cajas are important banking institutions in Spain, comparable to building societies in the UK. Their importance can be gauged from the fact that, while in 1977 the cajas held a market share of 32 per cent of all assets in the banking system, by 1991, this had risen to 41 per cent, with the graph continuing to show an upward trend in 1992. The principal characteristics of the cajas are as follows:

- They are usually associated with a particular area or region of Spain, and are crucial in the economic development of that region.
- They concentrate heavily on the savings and investment sectors of banking.
- Their customers are in the main private individuals or small and medium-sized companies.
- Their role and activities are more social in character than the banks.

The regional governments have been promoting the regional savings banks, and the trend is towards merger, with the biggest merger to date being between La Caixa and Caixa de Barcelona in July 1990, which

Table 4.4 *Top ten Spanish cajas (1992)*

Caja	Assets (million pesetas)	% Total
C A y Pensiones de Barcelona	5,013,108	21.63
C A y M P de Madrid	2,717,756	11.73
C A de Cataluña	1,055,759	4.56
Bilbao Bizkaia Kutxa	1,018,465	4.40
C A Del Mediterráneo	873,997	3.77
Bancaja	868,691	3.75
C A de Galicia	832,378	3.59
C A y M P de Zaragoza, Aragón y Rioja	817,972	3.53
Unicaja	786,124	3.39
C A M P de Gipuzkoa y S Sebastián	631,841	2.73

C A = Caja de ahorros
Source: *Anuario El País*

created the largest financial entity in Spain and the second largest savings bank in Europe, by deposits, after La Cassa di Rispermo delle Provincie Lombarde in Italy. The resulting caja has assets that in 1992 were greater than any of Spain's leading private banks (see Table 4.4).

Until recently the Cajas, almost all of which are regional or local in origin, have been limited by law to a certain geographical area. Although legislation now allows them to operate freely across the country, a new 1989 Law, the **Ley de Organos Rectores de Cajas de Ahorro** (LORCA), was designed by the Socialist government to have the eventual effect of handing over control of the cajas to the seventeen autonomous regional governments. The trend is already well established, with the number of cajas falling from eighty-two in 1978 to seventy-six in 1989 and to fifty-three at the end of 1992. The ultimate consequence of this would seem to be to reduce the fifty-three cajas existing in 1993 to one per region.

The cajas, assisted by the liberalization of the banking system, have become more openly aggressive and self-confident in recent years. They have 14,000 branches across Spain, with 42 per cent located in centres of population with fewer than 10,000 inhabitants, and they control about half the finance in the property market through mortgages and investments. The cajas have also begun to grasp the nettle of the wider European market by issuing customers with automatic till cards that can be used in other EC countries. In 1993, the cajas mounted a major summer campaign designed to win support away from the banks, investing 400 million pesetas on television, radio, newspaper and magazine advertising.

Stockmarkets

In the 1970s and 1980s, Spain's stock exchanges laboured under an antiquated structure, which goes a long way towards explaining why Spanish stockmarkets have been among the least active and least important in the Western world. Spain has three long-established exchanges in Madrid (1831), Bilbao (1915) and Barcelona (1915), and a recently opened exchange in Valencia (1980). Madrid accounts for about 80 per cent of all stockmarket transactions, Barcelona about 15 per cent, while Bilbao and Valencia between them represent a mere 5 per cent.

The traditional recourse of Spanish companies to the banking system for finance to expand meant relatively few transactions on the exchanges until the mid-1980s, when a series of reforms transformed the exchanges into modern entities with the latest technology. The process was initiated with a 1978 commission to examine ways in which to stimulate activity on the exchanges. Reforms that followed in the early 1980s were successful in persuading more companies to issue new shares as a means of generating more capital for expansion.

The reforms have led to greater decentralization, the establishment of a new body to oversee stockmarket transactions, and finally, in 1989, a law (the **Ley de Reforma del Mercado de Valores**) to streamline practices and bring them more into line with other Western exchanges. Early signs are that large investors have benefited most from the changes, amid greatly increased stockmarket activity, which has also attracted foreign investors to the Spanish exchanges. Foreign investors are free to invest but are only allowed to acquire up to 50 per cent of a company's stock. Larger stakes need special authorization.

Despite comparatively low levels of exchange activity, more Spaniards appear to be viewing the stockmarket as a good investment. In 1989, for instance, the average profit increase of firms quoted on the stockmarket was estimated to be 21 per cent, while a minimum annual rise of 12 per cent was predicted up to 1993. Banks and electrical firms comprise 60 per cent of all firms on the exchanges. A proliferation of real-estate companies in the late 1980s reflected the property boom in Spain.

While the total volume of business on the Spanish exchanges in 1991 was about the same level as 1990, with dividends rising by 17 per cent, 1992 was a difficult year for investors, with the Madrid exchange reaching its lowest point in October, following the ERM convulsions of September. By the end of the year, a partial recovery was in place, however. Three hundred and ninety-eight companies were quoted on the exchange at year end, representing a net loss of thirty-five during the year. Despite difficulties, dividends still increased again by 13.4 per cent, making stockmarket investment a healthy one. The Madrid exchange consolidated its position in 1992 as the fourth in Europe behind London, Frankfurt and Paris.

According to the 1988–89 OECD Economic Survey, the recent Spanish overhaul of the stock exchange, including the abolition of the monopoly position of brokers, had a favourable impact on the international community. The challenge ahead is for the Spanish stockmarkets to continue to liberalize and become more competitive internationally.

In the past few years six Spanish firms (three state-owned, three private) have taken the revolutionary step of entering Wall Street, with flotation on the US stock exchange. The three state-owned companies – Telefónica, Endesa and Repsol – have met with considerable success to date but the three private banking concerns – Banco Bilbao–Vizcaya, Banco Central and Banco de Santander – have encountered serious problems in appealing to US investors, apparently with long memories of the Latin American foreign debt crisis earlier in the 1980s, which ruined a number of US banks and which has left investors wary of 'Hispanic' banks ever since. However, the very fact of just 'being on Wall Street' is seen as prestige enough in Spanish quarters, and further evidence of Spain's desire to be part of the Western financial scene.

Insurance and pension funds

There has been a convergence of banking and insurance interests in Spain as the growth of life-insurance business has attracted banks, while the distribution networks of banks have attracted insurance companies. There are a large number of small insurance firms in Spain, many of them owned by the banks, although the insurance market, dominated by vehicle insurance, is quite small (total premiums in 1986 were only 2.2 per cent of GDP compared with a UK figure of 8 per cent). About one half of the industry is in the hands of foreigners, whether through overseas offices or participation in Spanish companies. Thus BUPA owns Sanitas; Norwich Union acquired Plus Ultra from BBV in 1990; and Scottish Widows began a joint venture in 1990 with Spain's second largest private medical insurer, Previasa. In 1991 and 1992, Spain's two biggest banks forged alliances with foreign insurers. First, Italy's Assurazioni Generali allied with the Banco Central Hispanoamericano to establish a joint venture second only in insurance premiums to Spain's biggest insurance group, Mapfre. Then the Banco Bilbao–Vizcaya joined forces with AXA of France to create Spain's fifth biggest insurance company. Foreign accountancy firms have also begun to penetrate the Spanish market, and the free movement promised by post-1992 Europe offers both threats and opportunities to Spanish insurance firms.

The insurance industry is at an expansionist stage, due to the prospects afforded by a market where there is an under-insurance mentality and where 40 per cent of Spaniards have not yet taken out a policy. The most frequent private insurance is comprehensive car insurance, arranged by 23 per cent of Spaniards, followed by home insurance at 22 per cent, health at 19 per cent, life at 15 per cent, pensions at 9 per cent and savings at 4 per cent. With regard to the total amount of premiums, Spain ranks in sixth position in the EC, with considerable scope for development. Foreign penetration is bound to continue increasing as indigenous insurance firms find it difficult to compete in the Single European Market.

An area in which the cajas are competing openly with banks is the pension funds market. It was estimated in 1989 that 60 per cent of pension-fund business is in the hands of the banks, 22 per cent with the cajas, and 10 per cent with insurance companies.

The dual appeal of pension funds is that dealing with them does not attract VAT and profits from investments do not attract company tax. The largest holdings are with the main banks especially BBV, Banco Central Hispanoamericano, Banco de Santander and Grupo March.

The trade unions (see pp. 75–76) have also entered the market, with the Socialist UGT establishing an insurance company and the Communist Workers' Commissions also setting up a pension fund company.

Conclusion

The progress made by Spain's financial institutions in the 1980s has been astonishing. The rate of technological updating by the banks, cajas and stock exchanges has been as rapid as the process of opening up to foreign competition, investment and acquisition. Furthermore, since the deposit guarantee fund was established, there is now a high level of security for depositors and institutions. The fund now extends to banks and cajas and guarantees each depositor the return of up to $1\frac{1}{2}$ million pesetas of savings in any banking institution in danger of collapse. No bank has gone under since the fund was created and cajas that have been in difficulty have been taken over by other cajas in a rationalization process of mutual benefit to the customer and the sector. Spain's banking institutions face up to the end of the century in a much better state of preparedness than seemed possible at the time of Franco's death in 1975. They will need to sustain the pace of modernization in a climate where the EC is planning legislation to bring banking and financial practices in all its member states into line.

5 Business and accountancy

Introduction

Until recently, regulation of business in Spain, although provided for in piecemeal legislation over a period of decades, was not particularly thorough. Many companies, in their business and accounting practices, did not apply scrupulous standards, and, as a consequence, a number of companies were susceptible to allegations of unfair operation. The liberalization of the economy, which began under Franco, but which accelerated in the subsequent transition to democracy, made it essential for the Spanish business culture literally and metaphorically to 'put its books in order'. EC membership made it equally necessary for Spanish accounting procedures to seek to emulate well-established procedures elsewhere in Europe. The process of rapprochement is still under way, but, crucially in the past few years, improved accounting practices have been made mandatory for Spanish firms. A statutory audit is now required for all except small companies. Auditors must be independent of the company and audits must be conducted by qualified professionals who are officially recognized by the Institute of Accounting and Auditing and included in the Institute's register. The climate therefore has changed dramatically since 1986, and further legislation is expected as the 1990s proceed.

Statutory requirements

Until recently, the statutory accounting requirements for Spanish companies were laid down by the 1973 **Plan General de Contabilidad** (general accounting plan), although this was modified by further legislation in the 1970s and 1980s that applied only to certain sectors of industry. A new accounting plan in 1990 drew the various strands of previous legislation together and laid down mandatory requirements for firms' accounting procedures. The main requirements are as follows:

- Three official accounting records must be kept by law and must be stamped by the Mercantile Registry: a **Diario** (journal); an **Inventarios y balance** (balance sheet) showing profit and loss account and supporting details, e.g. inventories, accounts receivable, etc; and **Actas** (minutes of directors' and shareholders' meetings).
- Bookkeeping records must be in Spanish, and the entries must be in chronological order and expressed in pesetas. The journal entries need only consist of monthly totals of movements if these are supported by sufficient detail in auxiliary unstamped records. This book, which must not be more than 4 months in arrears, must also include quarterly trial balances and year-end schedules of assets and liabilities. Bookkeeping records must be kept by firms for a period of 6 years from the last entry.
- Official books and records must comply with the relevant legal provisions of the 1990 law, since these books are the only accounting records recognized for official purposes. The rights of the company and its shareholders, tax declarations, liquidations, dividends, etc., are all based on the official books and records. It is possible however, for a company to apply to have its own accounting plan approved, the main requirement being that any such method should be adequate to produce the necessary information in the form required by the Spanish authorities.

In 1988, a new audit law was approved. It regulated the accounting profession, and determined that the filing of annual audited financial statements was mandatory (from 1990) for all firms of reasonable size, taking into consideration the volume of operations, the amount of total assets, number of employees and other activities e.g. financial intermediaries, banking and insurance arrangements, etc. Again, a number of statutory requirements were established with the main provisions as follows:

- Auditors must be appointed by the shareholders' general meeting before the end of the current financial year, to examine and report on the financial statements, distribution of profits and the directors' report. Only firms – usually small and medium-sized companies – that can present simplified accounts in a shortened version, are not obliged to appoint auditors.
- Auditors must be appointed for a minimum period of 3 years and maximum of 9 years. After the maximum period, auditors cannot be reappointed until a 3-year period has elapsed.
- A stock exchange regulation provides that companies quoted on the stock exchange must appoint independent auditors.
- Investment companies and investment funds held by companies require the appointment of auditors recognized by the **Instituto de**

Contabilidad y Auditoría de Cuentas (Institute of Accounting and Auditing), the Spanish government regulatory body. This body supervises the accounting profession, and checks the information that must be filed regularly with the Ministry of Economy and Finance.
- The tax authorities do not require audited financial statements.

Accounting principles

Compared with some other EC countries, there are relatively few specified accounting principles. The principles that now apply were laid down by the accounting legislation referred to above: the principles of accrual, cost, consistency, prudence, true and fair view, and going concern. Owing to the lack of established accounting principles, those principles required by tax legislation were to a great extent used in the past, especially in circumstances where recording items in the official accounting books could have had tax implications. The main investor considerations may therefore be summarized as follows:

- Financial statements are prepared from the general accounting records.
- Statutory accounting records are the bases for tax returns.
- Tax returns and financial statements overlap and complement each other considerably.
- Balance sheet and income statement are based on accepted accounting principles.
- Accounts must be kept on an accrual basis.
- Specified principles must be consistently applied.
- Changes in the method of valuation of assets require footnote disclosure.

Form and content of published accounts

Published accounts of major companies in Spain comprise three forms: the balance sheet, the income statement and the annual report.

Balance sheet

All companies are required to complete a full balance sheet, indicating assets and liabilities, although some smaller companies, with a total number of employees below fifty and with assets of less than 230 million pesetas or turnover of less than 480 million pesetas, are allowed to present a simplified balance sheet.

As a general rule, acquisition or production costs are the bases of valuation of assets and liabilities. Adjustments for valuations are permitted if they are based on a reasonable commercial appraisal, with a view to valuing them at the lowest cost corresponding to the closing date of the balance sheet. The lower valuation cannot be maintained if the reasons that motivate such adjustments cease to exist. The general accounting plan determines how certain assets and liabilities are valued, as follows:

- *Marketable securities.* These are valued at acquisition cost whether yielding fixed or varied income. The values of the securities consist of the total consideration paid to the seller, and include, where applicable, subscription rights and brokers' charges.
- *Inventories.* These are valued at whichever is the lower of cost or market value. Cost value includes invoiced amounts plus all additional expenses arising up to the point of arrival at the warehouse. Market value is defined as replacement cost or realizable value, with both the FIFO and LIFO methods of valuation acceptable.
- *Fixed assets.* These are valued at cost less accumulated depreciation, which in turn should be calculated on the basis of the estimated useful lives of the assets.
- *Foreign currency liabilities.* The exchange rate ruling at the time of incurring the debt determines the valuation, although exchange differences arising from currency fluctuations should be recorded when the related debt is paid.
- *Foreign currency assets.* The method of valuation is the same as for foreign currency liabilities.

The following are the reserves most commonly found in the balance sheets of Spanish companies:

1 *Legal reserve.* A minimum of 10 per cent of net profits must be transferred to a legal reserve until such reserve equals 20 per cent of the share capital. This reserve, while not exceeding that minimum limit, may only be used to offset losses.
2 *Voluntary reserve.* A voluntary reserve is the balance of retained earnings after allocation to the legal reserve. The total amount is available for distribution, provided the capital of the company is intact. This provision is necessary because it is Spanish practice, attributable partly to tax rules, to book losses in a separate 'intangible asset' account and not deduct them automatically from retained earnings. However, when the company's equity turns out to be lower than the share capital of the company, the current profit will automatically be used to compensate the equity.
3 *Share premium reserve.* Premiums received on the issue of the company's own shares are treated as a voluntary reserve, and may be capitalized or distributed.

4   *Regularization reserves.* These arise generally from the revaluation of fixed assets and reference should be made to the specific legislation in each case to determine the purpose for which these reserves may be used.

Income statement

This statement normally consists of four separate accounts, as follows:

- *Trading account.* This usually includes income from normal trading or commercial operations and the costs, both direct and indirect, incurred in generating such income.
- *Account of non-trading operations.* This includes income and expenditure other than those related to the trading account, plus any extraordinary items.
- *Investment portfolio account.* This account registers the net gains or losses resulting from sales of investments and subscription rights, as well as dividend and interest income.
- *Profit and loss account.* This account summarizes the results of the three accounts above and reflects the corporate tax charge where applicable, amounts allocated to certain provisions and the appropriations to reserves and dividends.

Annual report

This report, which appears as notes to the accounts, complements and comments on the balance sheet and on the income statement. The annual report should contain indications of the criteria used for valuation, in addition to stating the source of funds and how the funds have been used. The report, as in other EC countries, will normally outline the economic position of the company and its future prospects.

Accounting profession

The Institute of Accounting and Auditing, as outlined above (see p. 52), is now the principal body with responsibility for co-ordinating the profession, for formulating national accounting principles, and for advising government on all areas within the domain of accounting. It is, however, a more recent organization than the **Instituto de Censores Jurados de Cuentas**, an older professional accounting body.

The **Asociación Española de Contabilidad y Administración de Empresas** (Association for Accounting and Company Administration) was founded by prominent members from the accounting profession, industry and the universities. The Association promotes technical competence in accounting standards and business management and provides a forum for research into and discussion of matters of topical interest.

Public sector accounting

The Spanish parliament delegates the detailed examination and control over all public sector accounts to an Audit Tribunal, which was entrusted by the Constitution with responsibility for the financial scrutiny of all state and public sector accounts. A number of regional governments, notably Catalonia and Galicia, have now created their own audit tribunals without prejudice to the power of the state Audit Tribunal, which seeks to confirm whether the various public bodies have legally and efficiently discharged their responsibilities in accordance with the constitution and the law. It presents an annual report either to the Spanish parliament or to the legislative assemblies of the regional governments. It is an independent body, whose members have the same status as members of the judiciary. They have to be suitably qualified as auditors, lawyers or economists, with a minimum of 15 years' professional experience.

Whereas in the past state-owned companies, especially within the INI group, employed their own audit section, it is now usual for publicly owned firms to have external audits by independent auditors usually drawn from the major international accounting firms. This reflects an increased reliance on external foreign sources of finance and the need to indicate creditworthiness, as well as being a measure of the increasing movement of state enterprises into foreign trade.

EC influence

Since Spain joined the EC in 1986, accounting legislation has been extensively revised to bring Spain into line with EC directives. The main results of this process have been the new general accounting plan, which establishes new accounting principles and the form and content of published accounts; the new audit law regulating the accounting profession; and the reform of mercantile legislation (corporation law, company law and commercial code), which introduced major changes relating to the annual accounting records, the rules of valuation of assets, the accounting of consolidated statements, and the statutory audit requirements.

Spanish accounting professionals still await eagerly, although with some apprehension, to see whether and how promised EC job mobility for their profession will affect their career and employment prospects.

Conclusion

Recent legislation has injected an element of fairness and accounting rectitude into the presentation of published accounts in Spain. This has taken place within the context of a reorganization and modernization of Spanish financial institutions and markets (see Chapter 4). Despite the uncertainties of post-1992 Europe, it is inevitable that the process of reform will continue as Spain's business culture strives forcefully to attain the levels and standards set by her EC partners.

6 Business and the labour market

Introduction

The principal factors providing the background to the labour market are located in Spain's rapid industrialization since the 1960s, set against the authoritarian isolationism of the Franco dictatorship. Thus a massive exodus of workers from Franco's Spain, which began with the close of the Civil War in 1939, when an estimated half a million left the country as political refugees, was to be supplemented in the decades that followed by a continuing haemorrhage of manpower seeking employment in the more developed countries of Europe, as well as in the USA and Latin America. In 1989, 2,800,000 Spaniards still worked in these countries, providing much needed revenue for their home country.

Alongside emigration, the 1950s, 1960s and 1970s also witnessed wholescale domestic migration from the countryside to the towns and from the agricultural, poorer areas, such as Extremadura and Andalusia, to the more prosperous urban environments of Barcelona, Madrid and Bilbao.

As in other countries, Spanish women began to enter the workforce for the first time in the 1960s, and unemployment, in the early post-Franco years of the democratic transition, began to soar, illustrating the human cost of Franco's failure to modernize Spain's economic infrastructure. Spain's business culture is still struggling to come to terms with the impact on the labour market that the sea-changes of the past three decades have generated on a population that in mid-1990 stood at 38,870,000.

Demographic trends – general

Spain has one of the lowest population densities in Western Europe, with the average of 78 inhabitants per square kilometre, a little higher than densities in Greece and Ireland, but only one-sixth of The Netherlands. The 50 million annual foreign visitors also have to be taken into account.

Table 6.1   *Major urban centres of population*

Madrid	3.1 million
Barcelona	1.7 million
Valencia	0.7 million
Seville	0.7 million
Zaragoza	0.6 million
Malaga	0.6 million
Bilbao	0.4 million
Las Palmas (Canaries)	0.4 million
Valladolid	0.3 million
Murcia	0.3 million
Palma (Balearics)	0.3 million
Cordoba	0.3 million

Source: *Avance del Anuario Estadístico de España, 1989*

Unequal population distribution has created a regional imbalance. There has been a growing trend towards major concentrations on the coast and in several clusters in the interior, notably Madrid. Heavy depopulation of the interior has left thousands of dead or deserted villages across the country as young people move to the conurbations for jobs. Forty per cent of the population live in towns of over 10,000 inhabitants while there are fifty municipalities with populations over 100,000. In 1900, there were only 220 towns in Spain with a population over 10,000, but this had risen to 604 towns by 1991. If one classifies towns with a population over 10,000 as urban, then the full extent of Spain's urbanization this century is apparent: in 1900, 32 per cent of the population was urban, but, in 1991, the figure was 73 per cent. Population figures for the main towns and for the regions are given in Table 6.1 and Table 6.2.

Between 1900 and 1991, the largest growing regions in population terms were, in order: Madrid, Catalonia, the Basque Country, the Canaries, Valencia and the Balearics. The regions that have suffered the highest demographic loss were, in order: Castile–Leon, Galicia, Castile–La Mancha, Extremadura, Aragon. The figures highlight the massive rural exodus and the rise of regions with large industrial conurbations alongside regions made prosperous by tourism.

The single biggest concern for Spain is a fall in the birthrate more dramatic than that in virtually any other European country (see Table 6.3). In 1964, live births per 1,000 inhabitants stood at 21.9 but, by 1991, this had fallen to 11.2. The downward graph really dates back to 1975. In 1975, the average number of children per woman in Spain was 2.8, but, by 1991, this had fallen to below 1.4, a fertility rate below the level needed to replace generations. The figures demonstrate that women in

Table 6.2 *Population by region*

Andalusia	7.1 million
Catalonia	6.1 million
Madrid	5.0 million
Valencia	3.9 million
Galicia	2.9 million
Castile–Leon	2.6 million
Basque Country	2.1 million
Castile–La Mancha	1.7 million
Canaries	1.6 million
Aragon	1.2 million
Asturias	1.1 million
Extremadura	1.1 million
Murcia	1.1 million
Balearics	0.8 million
Cantabria	0.5 million
Navarre	0.5 million
La Rioja	0.3 million

Source: Municipal Register, 1989

Table 6.3 *Growth of Spanish population*

	1971–80	*1981–90*
Births	6,491,778	4,536,900
Deaths	2,943,692	3,083.947
Natural growth	3,548,086	1,452,953
Emigration Balance	245,000	433,000
Total growth	3,793,086	1,885,953

Source: Instituto Nacional del Empleo

Spain are having fewer children, later, and that more are joining the workforce. In fact, four out of every five new job-seekers are women, although only a third of Spanish women constitute part of the workforce, again one of the lowest levels in Europe.

Social factors are obviously an important contributory factor, with fewer marriages in Spain in the 1980s and with the legalization of divorce in 1981, and abortion (under certain legally defined circumstances) in 1985. While every survey conducted indicates that cohabitation and sex before marriage are now widely accepted, despite being religiously taboo in traditional Spain, it is nonetheless the case that a mere 20,000 marriages a year end in divorce and that illegitimate births constitute only 7 per cent of the total.

The increase in deaths is due to a growing ageing population. Life expectancy, however, rose 2 years in the 1980s and more over-65s are living longer. One quarter of all Spaniards, however, are under the age of sixteen. Since 1975, with the restoration of democracy and following the first oil crisis, more Spanish emigrés returned to Spain. Now the flow of returnees is practically exhausted and relatively few Spaniards are emigrating. Spain is now a country of immigration: between 1981 and 1990, net entries (difference between entries and departures) of legal immigrants was estimated at 300,000, with an estimated 130,000 illegal immigrants. Thus, Spain is now experiencing similar phenomena, demographically, to other EC countries.

Demographic trends – Madrid

The drop in the number of young people in the 15–19 age group in Madrid since 1981 is almost certainly paralleled in other principal urban areas of Spain (for which, however, no information is available) and represents a nationwide problem that threatens business recruitment in the labour market as well as the vitality of Spain's main business centres (Table 6.4).

From 1981 to 1986, Madrid lost 100,000 inhabitants in total, while the average age increased from 31.6 years to 36.8 years. By the year 2000, Madrid is expected to have half the 15–19 age group that it had in 1986, with a predominance of over-65s. Madrid's birth rate, symptomatic of urban Spain as a whole, has fallen by a third in the last 10 years to 1.4 children per couple, one of the lowest of any capital city in Western Europe.

Table 6.4   *Madrid – fall in numbers of young people, 1981–2001*

	15–29 age (000s)	*15–19 age (000s)*
1981	741	293
1986	778	269
1991	787	241
1996 (projected)	696	189
2001 (projected)	568	141

Source: Boletín Estadístico de Madrid

Madrid's problem has prompted central and local government initiatives to counter the drift away from the major conurbations. The Mayor of Madrid, Juan Barranco, fears the trend could destroy the essential fabric of town centres in Spain and states, 'It could leave us with a centre of offices and shops, heavily depopulated, with only an ageing wealthy residential class'.

One of the main reasons for the population exodus is the spectacular rise in housing prices, which has driven young people in particular to live in dormitory towns hours away from the centre or to abandon urban living altogether. The boom in house prices has meant an increase in new-build up-market housing, inaccessible to most of the labour market, but the virtual disappearance of municipal housebuilding. For those entering the job market or those on low incomes in the first years of employment, the only alternative for the majority of young people is to remain in the family home, and 20 per cent of married couples, at the end of 1986, were living with parents. The housing crisis has resulted in severe overcrowding, with Madrid's 3.5 persons per dwelling one of the highest levels of any European capital. A vicious circle has now emerged, with 62 per cent of males in Madrid between the ages of 25 and 29 unmarried in 1986 (compared with 48 per cent in 1981). A similar trend for women further accentuates the decline in the birthrate.

Labour market trends

In 1960, 39 per cent of the Spanish working population in civilian employment were employed in agriculture. By 1991, this figure had fallen to 12 per cent, a level equivalent to Spain's Mediterranean EC partners but still significantly higher than France, with 7 per cent employed in agriculture, Germany with 5 per cent and the United Kingdom with 2 per cent.

Spain's manufacturing workforce changed very little in this period, from a much lower base, with 24 per cent employed in manufacturing in 1991, as in 1960. This figure can be compared with France (22 per cent), Germany (32 per cent), and the United Kingdom (24 per cent).

Spain, like all of its EC partners, saw a continuing rapid expansion of employment in services between 1960 and 1991, although the scale of growth in Spain was even higher than in other countries. Thus, in Spain between 1960 and 1991, the percentage employed in services increased from 31 per cent to 54 per cent. (In France employment in this sector rose from 40 per cent to 62 per cent, in Germany from 39 per cent to 54 per cent and in the United Kingdom from 48 per cent to 68 per cent.) Agriculture now accounts for 5.2 per cent of GDP. Manufacturing, mining and the utilities account for 30 per cent, while construction accounts for 8 per cent and services 57 per cent (see Table 6.5).

Table 6.5   *Spanish civilian employment (1991)*

By sector	(%)	GDP at factor cost by origin (%)
Agriculture	12	5
Industry	24	30
Construction	10	8
Services	54	57

Source: OECD

The proportion of women in the active population also increased dramatically between 1960, when the figure was 20.1 per cent, to 1991, when the proportion was 33.3 per cent. The trend continues to accelerate, but Spain still has some considerable way to go to emulate the place of women in employment achieved by her Northern EC partners.

The Spanish labour market has traditionally been characterized by a rigid legal framework and work practices. Job security was very tight, and large redundancy payments necessary if a contract was broken. Until the mid-1980s, it was difficult for employers to use part-time or fixed-term contracts. In addition, there was and still is a substantial **economía sumergida** (black, or submerged, economy), with perhaps 2 million people employed in a variety of sectors, but especially service industries, construction, and manufacturing industries such as textiles, food, toys and shoes.

Since 1984, the Spanish government has been gradually introducing greater flexibility into the labour market, perceiving the need for Spain to come into line with other EC countries over employment legislation. The advent of the Single European Market has accelerated this trend. The period up to 1992 has thus seen the introduction of fixed-term contracts, usually for 6 months, the spread of part-time employment, especially for the under-25s and over-45s, and expansion of training schemes and more provision for early retirement. These have been accompanied by special employment programmes to promote small industry and self-employment, which include employment and training grants, relief from social security contributions, fiscal measures and soft loans.

The result has been an explosion in temporary jobs, with an estimated one in three of the workforce on such contracts in 1992. Four in five of workers under the age of 20 fall into this category. Whereas in 1985, one year after the first major measures to improve flexibility in employment laws had been implemented, only 11 per cent of employees were on temporary contracts, in 1992 the figure was over 30 per cent. The government claims that new flexibility has created 2 million jobs.

Further flexibility in the labour market has ensued from a government report in 1990, which made a number of recommendations. Temporary posts may now be for a minimum of 3 months instead of 6, and a maximum of 2 years instead of 3. A new kind of apprenticeship, known as a **contrato en prácticas**, is available for a minimum of 6 months for those with further educational qualifications. **Centros de formación** (training centres) have been set up nationally to assist the unemployed, while temporary posts have been created for the over-45 age group and for the disabled. Part-time employment has been on the increase in an effort to alleviate redundancies and cuts in full-time employment.

Working practices in firms have had to change also as Spanish firms become more absorbed into international markets. Many Spanish companies, especially the larger ones, have had to recognize the need for new communications with the workforce, both vertical and horizontal, the need for review of remuneration and for job evaluation generally, and the need for more workforce skills training. Most strikingly, as companies invest in new plant and technology, the training emphasis in Spain has switched dramatically to training for young people in the new technologies.

Unemployment

Spain's dramatic transition from dictatorship to democracy has been accompanied by the highest rates of unemployment seen in OECD countries, as Spain's economy has undergone the severest adjustments (Tables 6.6 and 6.7).

The very acute employment crisis of the 1980s was caused by many factors, including:

- A slowdown in economic growth through the 1970s exacerbated by the oil shocks and the uncertain political climate.
- A vigorous surge in wage costs following Franco's death in 1975.
- A marked deterioration in fixed investment in the 1970s.
- Delays in adjusting production structures.

From 1974, when employment stood at a record level, to 1982, employment fell by over 2 million, and a further fall of 1,900,000 was registered between 1983 and 1986. By 1985, also, the participation rate, i.e. the ratio of employment to population of working age, had fallen to 43.7 per cent, the lowest level of any industrialized country. As early as 1978, Spain's unemployment rate topped the EC average, and, in 1985, climbed above 21 per cent, i.e. twice as high as EC member states. In addition, the length of time for which people remained unemployed and the

Table 6.6   *Spanish unemployment rates, 1977–93*

Year	(%)
1977	5.2
1978	6.9
1979	8.5
1980	11.2
1981	13.9
1982	15.8
1983	17.2
1984	20.0
1985	21.4
1986	21.0
1987	20.1
1988	19.1
1989	16.9
1990	16.3
1991	16.3
1992	18.4
1993	22.7

Source: OECD

composition of unemployment by age and sex were both unfavourable to Spain. Thus, the proportion of long-term unemployed, i.e. for 12 months or more, at 54.2 per cent in 1986, was higher than that of all other EC partners, with the exception of the Benelux countries. Youth unemployment (16–24 age group) at 47.5 per cent was also the highest in the OECD in 1987, and compared at the time with the United Kingdom at 33.6 per cent, France at 33 per cent and former West Germany at 22.7 per cent.

A breakdown of the unemployment rate in 1987, compared with an already poor 1981 (Table 6.7), illustrates the severity of the problem facing Spain in the late 1980s. Owing to the economic policies pursued by the government outlined earlier, (see pp. 2–5), however, the unemployment problem began to turn around in 1987 and especially 1988.

While the agricultural labour force continued to decline, 400,000 new jobs were created in other sectors in the late 1980s, a net increase in the number of employed of 300,000 or 3 per cent. Employment growth in the construction sector was running at three times previous levels. In the service sector, female employment grew twice as fast as male employment, while the female participation rate increased from an average of 29.3 per cent in the 1983–5 period to 32.5 per cent in 1988. Next to

Table 6.7 *Unemployment breakdown (1981 and 1987)*

	1981 (%)	1987 (%)
Male	13.0	16.8
Female	17.5	28.0
Under 25 years	34.3	43.0
25–54 years	9.3	15.0
Over 55 years	5.7	9.4

Source: OECD

Ireland, though, female participation rates were still the lowest in the OECD.

Also in the early 1990s, greater flexibility in the labour market resulted from a number of employment promotion programmes in firms, sponsored by the government, which initially created many thousands of temporary and part-time jobs. About half of these jobs have, however, since been converted to permanent contracts, with the assistance of tax changes designed to encourage firms to create new permanent forms of employment.

Male unemployment fell by 1.6 percentage points between 1987 and 1988. Youth unemployment, significantly, had the sharpest reduction, mainly due to the special employment programmes, although at 40 per cent the 16–24 age group still compared poorly with the 25–54 age group, at 13.5 per cent. Also in 1988 and 1989, further evidence of economic growth in Spain finally influencing the job market was provided by a reversal in the earlier steep upward trend in long-term unemployment. In 1991, unemployment began to fall below 16 per cent in Spain for the first time since 1982, but by the year end, had closed at 16.3 per cent. This figure, though a marked improvement on the mid-1980s, was still intractably high compared with 6.8 per cent for the OECD as a whole.

By 1992, it was evident that the tremendous gains in employment since the mid-1980s were being reversed as Spain began to feel the effects of an international recession, perhaps 2 years later than the UK, France and Germany. Unemployment rose in 1992 to 18.4 per cent, compared with 16.3 per cent in 1991, and the OECD calculated a figure of 22.7 per cent for year end 1993. The scale of the turnaround is clear in the figures for job creation: in 1989, 490,000 net jobs were created; there were 211,600 in 1990 and 60,900 in 1991; but, in 1992, there was a net loss in jobs of 412,970. The construction industry saw the highest number of job losses as public works contracts subsided after Expo '92 and the Olympics.

A more detailed analysis of the unemployment figures for 1992 shows that 60 per cent of registered unemployed were female (49 per cent for the EC as a whole) and that the female unemployment rate of 26 per cent (12 per cent in the EC) was almost double the male unemployment rate of 14 per cent. Unemployment in the under-25 age group fell slightly during 1991 but still accounted for 35 per cent of all unemployed at the end of 1992. The problem of unemployment in Spain is particularly difficult for young people leaving school or college and seeking their first job; the unemployment rate among this group was more than 30 per cent, compared with an EC average of 18 per cent. The European Commission, in July 1993, called upon the Spanish government to take 'special measures' to tackle unemployment, pointing out that Spain was one of the EC members that had created the fewest jobs from the economic expansion of the 1980s, along with Ireland and Greece.

Unemployment training schemes

Additional to government employment programmes outlined earlier, the **National Institute for Employment** (INEM) has been devoting increasing resources (70,000 million pesetas in 1989) to training for the unemployed. Centres have been established throughout Spain but especially in areas affected by industrial 'reconversion'. Emphasis has been upon training in the new technologies and on collaborative ventures with the trade unions. INEM has worked also in close conjunction with regional governments and with the European Commission, since it derives half of its budget from the European Social Fund. Further detail on training is provided in Chapter 9 (see pp. 90–91).

Conclusion

The Spanish labour market, after decades of rapid and often painful readjustments to Spain's developing economy, now faces a further difficult period of high unemployment. A survey published by the Bank of Spain in 1993 revealed that the widespread nature of unemployment was affecting the pattern of domestic migration. No longer were people moving from one region to another in search of employment as in previous decades. Now people were tending to stay in their region of origin, and moving to other regions only for professional promotion or to improve their quality of life. Family and personal circumstances are increasingly influencing the decision to stay at home or move, although variations in house prices or wage and salary levels are important factors as well. In other words, the labour market in Spain in the 1990s is beginning to resemble the labour markets of other EC countries after experiencing a twentieth-century industrial revolution.

7 Business and trade unions

Introduction

A crucial element in Spanish business culture has been the development in the last two decades of a free trade-union structure, from the ruins of an undemocratic system of 'vertical syndicates' under Franco, in which everyone who worked was obliged to be a member of one of twenty-eight vertical syndicates, arranged by industry, and constructed hierarchically to include all employees from top management to shopfloor worker. There was central control of the system, with the Minister for Syndical Relations a member of Franco's nominated government. The essentially undemocratic nature of the system can be gauged by the fact that as late as 1971 only 391 people were eligible to vote directly for the President of the Metal Workers' Syndicate, although the union had 1,300,000 members.

The collapse of vertical syndicalism, undermined from within by the Communist trade union, the **Comisiones Obreras** (Workers' Commissions) and from without by the unassailable march towards political pluralism, paved the way for a free trade-union structure, which since the late 1970s has had an increasing influence on the business culture. Led by the Workers' Commissions and the Socialist UGT (General Union of Workers), the trade unions initially, in a period where many companies had to learn how to negotiate with genuine worker representatives, adopted in the early 1980s a policy of conciliation and consensus, exemplified by the signing of a number of social and economic pacts with government and/or employers' confederations.

In the late 1980s, increasing disillusion with government monetary and fiscal policies, which accepted very high levels of unemployment and appeared to strike at workers' purchasing power, saw the unions turn towards open conflict with government and employers, a process culminating in Spain's first general strike for 50 years on 14 December 1988. Continuing trade-union malaise underlay the general election of 29 October 1989, which, with only the narrowest overall majority for Felipe González's Socialist government, left the necessity for early government/

employers/trade unions conciliation high on the new government's agenda.

Despite talks, however, trade union disillusion with government policies continued in the early 1990s. A further half-day general strike took place in May 1992 as a protest against the government's decision to reduce its budget deficit by cutting unemployment benefit, part of a government strategy to meet the convergence terms set by the EC Maastricht summit of December 1991. The half-day strike was not as successful as the 1988 general strike, as Spain's workforce became increasingly concerned by the return of mounting unemployment, a major factor in the 6 June 1993 general election, which returned González's government without an overall majority.

Industrial democracy – recent history

Evolution of free trade unions from the vertical syndicates took place in the 1960s and 1970s, with Franco still in power, as employers increasingly began to negotiate with genuine though illegal workers' representatives rather than through the official vertical organization. Although present-day trade unions have had only a brief modern history, the four decades of Francoism were unable to erase completely from collective memory an earlier period at the start of the present century and up to the 1930s in which Spanish trade unions were among the largest and the most powerful in the Western world. Industrial democracy's recent history has a number of important benchmarks:

Late 1950s/ early 1960s   The birth of the Communist trade union, Workers' Commissions, as an illegal and clandestine movement, to infiltrate the official vertical syndicates. Quickly spreads throughout Spain to assume national importance.

1962   The first big demonstration of nascent free trade unionism, with a Miners' strike in the North of Spain leading to Franco declaring a state of emergency.

1968   A report of the International Labour Organization (ILO) acknowledges the primacy of the illegal free trade-union movement.

1960s/ 1970s   Internal rebirth of the Socialist trade union, the UGT, helped by the rise of González's Socialist party.

1975   The last Franco government tinkers with vertical syndicalism to allow for emergent trade unions, but the attempt fails.

1975–7   Increasing industrial unrest as free trade unions demand abolition of vertical syndicates.

1977   Legalization of free trade unions and abolition of vertical syndicates.

Table 7.1 *Spanish industrial disputes, 1966–80*

Year	No. strikes	Man-hours lost
1966	205	1,785,492
1970	817	6,750,900
1975	855	10,355,120
1976	1,568	110,016,240
1977	994	92,572,050
1978	1,356	128,738,478
1979	1,789	171,067,049
1980	1,669	108,625,662

Source: *Confederación Española de Organizaciones Empresariales* (Spanish Employers' Confederation)

1978 First trade-union elections to choose workers' delegates in firms.
1980 Workers' statute becomes law. The statute lays down workers' rights, representation and collective bargaining procedures. A minimum wage level is to be fixed annually by the government in consultation with unions and employers. Works' committees are established as the effective voice of the workforce in companies, able to negotiate with employers over working conditions and over wages, although local, regional or national wage negotiations will usually determine the parameters.

The tremendous pressure exerted by the workforce on the fragile democracy that was emerging in Spain in the mid-1970s is obvious when one examines the strike record and the number of man-hours lost as a result in the period from 1966 up to 1980. The ten-fold increase in man-hours lost between 1975 and 1976 is the most telling indicator of the Spanish people's reaction to Franco's death, although, as can be seen from Table 7.1, the figure continued to mount to a peak of 171,067,049 hours lost in 1979.

Social and economic pacts

The fact that strikes in 1980 were still at a high level despite a reduction from 1979 was probably caused by two main factors: works' committees initially had insufficient power to represent workers' interests, being restricted to negotiating over health and safety issues; and many Spanish firms were incredibly slow to recognize the reality of the changing situation, and instead of engaging in direct dialogue with the workforce, asked government for greater protection for their industries. Such dilatoriness merely encouraged workers to join unions and formulate demands.

A developing battle between the Communist Workers' Commissions and the Socialist UGT was exacerbated by a bilateral agreement in 1980 signed between the UGT and the Spanish Employers' Confederation, the CEOE, a historic pact (the **AMI**), the first ever in Spain between employers and a national union. The main points of the pact were that wage rises of between 13 per cent and 16 per cent in profit-making companies would be paid and works' committees in each firm were to have access to company balance sheets and to be consulted in any management decision on employment policy, productivity, working methods or conditions.

During 1980, the AMI pact was on the whole a success, with widespread adherence to the wage rise guidelines, and the UGT negotiating successfully to halt potentially major strikes in the car industry and the dockyards. The pact also paved the way for a new agreement, known as the **ANE**, in which the Workers' Commissions joined the UGT, the Employers' Confederation and the government as co-signatories. This pact, which was to last until the end of 1982, kept wage rises to 10.5 per cent maximum (with inflation running at a rate of about 15 per cent), modernized collective bargaining procedures, and secured promises from the government to improve employment and social-security provision. A further agreement, (the **AI**), this time between the unions and employers alone, extended co-operation into 1984, when the most far-reaching of the agreements to date was signed, the Economic and Social Accord (**AES**), a tripartite agreement between the UGT, management and the first Socialist government of Felipe González.

The Accord, covering 1985 and 1986, was important because it was the first of the agreements in which the government negotiated public spending plans with both sides of industry. Divided into two parts, the first part of the Accord detailed government commitments, and the second part was a legally binding agreement between the signatories. The main components of the first part were:

- A government promise to create 190,000 jobs in 1985, via increased public-sector funding and extra stimulus for private industry.
- A 'solidarity fund' of £284 million, raised by equal contributions from workers, employers and government, to support training and retraining schemes and innovatory job-creation projects, along the same lines as the EC's European Social Fund.

- An increase in personal allowances, the removal of more low-income earners from the tax net, and an extension of unemployment benefit from the 25 per cent eligible in 1984 to 48 per cent by the end of 1986.
- A government allocation of £237 million for investment in labour-intensive sectors to modernize plant and machinery.

The second part of the Accord applied to around 5 million workers covered by collective agreements in the public and private sectors and comprised:

- A pay increase band of between 5.5 per cent and 7.5 per cent.
- An agreement to increase productivity, and reduce absenteeism and systematic overtime by eradicating the common practice in Spain of multiple employment or double-jobbing.
- A rationalization programme to reduce the number of collective agreements signed at individual company level (3,500 running in 1984) by introducing more national and regional bargaining.
- A new system for resolving disputes through voluntary mediation and arbitration.

Since 31 December 1986, when the Accord terminated, no new pact has been signed in Spain, and there is substantial evidence of growing trade-union disenchantment with government economic policies. Whereas the Workers' Commissions refused to sign the Accord, the UGT later came to condemn its sister Socialist party in government for increasing job losses and eroding purchasing power. The Accord can be said, though, to have been successful in maintaining wage moderation, and a symptom of its success, paradoxically, is the mounting social disruption and political uncertainty that followed in the late 1980s and early 1990s when no pact was in place.

Trade unions' power battle in firms

The battle between the Communist Workers' Commissions and the Socialist UGT has centred around trade-union elections in which the workforce select delegates on works' committees to negotiate with management. The balance of power between the unions is shown in Table 7.2.

The election results show the rise of the UGT through the 1980s, although the picture after 1990 tends to mask a switch in allegiance in large firms of 100 employees upwards from the UGT to Workers' Commissions. The Communist union also won twice as many votes as the UGT in the telephone and telecommunications industry, and scored major

Table 7.2   *Spanish trade-union elections*

Trade union	Percentage of delegates elected to works' committees				
	1978	*1980*	*1982*	*1986*	*1990*
	%	%	%	%	%
Workers' Commissions	34.4	30.9	33.4	34.3	36.5
UGT	21.7	29.3	36.7	40.2	44.0
USO (Workers' Syndical Union)	3.9	8.7	4.6	3.8	2.8
Regional Unions	1.0	3.4	4.5	3.5	4.4
Others/independents	38.9	27.7	20.8	17.6	12.3

Source: Ministerio de Trabajo y Segaridad Social

successes in other crucial industries, including gas and energy, the railways and the banks. The UGT performed well in the 1986 and 1990 elections in small and medium-sized firms and in the tobacco industry, its only stronghold among large firms. This was surprising, given the fact that, in September 1986, the Socialist government had provided its UGT ally with a £21 million subsidy (and over 100 buildings) for its election campaign, representing the return of union assets seized by the Franco régime after the Civil War. The Workers' Commissions, having emerged only in the late 1950s, received practically nothing.

Trade union/government conflict

Increasing industrial unrest in 1987 and 1988, following the breakdown of the AES, the last social compact, reflected growing union anger at the effects of government policy, and culminated in a general strike on 14 December 1988.

In the years preceding the strike the Socialist government, in the view of the unions, had been accommodating the demands of employers, to achieve greater flexibility of labour. For instance, the government introduced 6-month, fixed-term contracts in firms as a means of creating new jobs, and proposed to abolish the statutory minimum wage for workers aged 18–24, to reduce redundancy payments and to extend part-time labour. At the same time Spain's low labour costs were being advertised as a national asset as the government attempted to attract multinational enterprises and foreign investment. According to the US business magazine *Fortune*, in 1987, 'labour costs in Spain are mouth-watering'. Some firms expected to pay Spanish workers up to 30 per cent less than workers elsewhere in Western Europe. Ford's Valencia plant, in which the UGT enjoys a major presence, had the lowest costs of any of the company's eight European factories.

In the absence of a new social pact, the UGT has been in bitter conflict with the government since 1987. The UGT opposed González's decision to keep Spain within NATO, UGT MPs voted against the government over pension legislation and, finally, the UGT leader, Nicolás Redondo, resigned his parliamentary seat in protest at the 1988 budget.

A 1988 UGT report on Spain's economy from 1977 to 1987 spent 300 pages condemning the government for a 'monetarist and fiscal policy more conservative than Helmut Kohl or Margaret Thatcher'. In contrast to the UGT report, the Spanish Employers' Confederation (CEOE) has been enthusiastic in its support for government policies, with José María Cuevas, the Confederation's President, declaring in 1988, 'the government should continue to fight inflation, improve firms' competitiveness and bring more flexibility into the labour market'. The trade unions' complete disillusion with government policies led inexorably to a general strike in 1988.

The 1988 general strike and its aftermath

The general strike of 14 December 1988 was monumentally successful, with two-thirds of Spain's workforce supporting the strike and paralyzing the country. The trigger for the strike was the government's youth employment plan, which sought to allocate £15,000 million to firms to engage unemployed workers below the age of 25 on short-term contracts at the minimum wage level. The UGT condemned the plan as 'the worst attack on workers since the Franco era', arguing that it would not solve the long-term unemployment problem. Redondo complained that 'only 18 per cent of jobs in Spain's expanding textile industry are permanent and over 30 per cent of production is in the hidden economy'. The labour market, he argued, has become 'the law of the jungle'.

Young workers in Spain form a reserve army for a huge black economy that some estimates put as high as 15 per cent or 20 per cent of legal GDP. Of every two people unemployed in Spain, one is between the ages of 16 and 25. There were over 1,400,000 in this category at the start of the 1990s and over 800,000 who had never had a job.

Following the success of the general strike, the UGT and Workers' Commissions agreed to meet Felipe González only if five prior conditions were met: scrapping the youth employment plan; compensating employees in state-owned industries and pensioners for their 2 per cent drop in real earnings in 1988; increasing to 48 per cent the number of jobless entitled to unemployment pay; recognizing civil servants' right to collective bargaining; and bringing the minimum pension into line with the minimum wage. These demands are only some of a whole battery of social and economic measures the unions have been pressing on government since 1989 to redistribute wealth, protect employees and expand trade-union rights and participation in the management of industry. The unions contend that when Spanish companies made low profits in the early 1980s, the workforce tightened its belt to boost profitability. Now that profits are higher, they argue, the workforce deserves its share.

Throughout 1989 and 1990, there was an impasse between the unions and government, with the Socialist party even threatening to set up its own trade union in competition with its long-time ally, the UGT. Most importantly the general strike saw the greatest co-operation yet between Spain's two main trade unions, determined to increase the union movement's power to the level of some of her neighbouring countries. The task is a difficult one in an economy based mainly on hundreds of thousands of small firms, and where trade union membership is between 20 per cent and 25 per cent of the working population. As one UGT leader commented, 'With such low membership the unions are left out of the major economic decisions made in Spain. Most of the government's plans for the economy we learn about through the newspapers!'

A further half-day general strike in May 1992 clearly indicated mounting trade-union anger at government economic measures announced shortly after the Maastricht summit, to reduce Spain's budget deficit by capping health spending, ending public sector bail-outs, and reducing unemployment provisions. Although support for the strike was half-hearted, workers in a number of key industries took direct action in 1992, which embarrassed a government obsessed by Spain's international image in the year of Expo and the Olympics. A refuse collectors' strike in the spring of 1992 left the Madrid metro and airport awash with litter just as the capital city was embarking upon its year as the European Capital of Culture! More seriously, coalminers in Asturias, accustomed to defying right-wing and fascist regimes for generations, mounted a violent strike aimed at EC policies and the government they helped to elect, ignoring their own union's demands to return to work. Clearly job losses were again high on the political agenda.

The trade unions continued to mount pressure upon the government in the run-up to the June 1993 general election, demanding that unemployment should be the first priority of a new government. The trade-union leaders therefore were happy to sit down with González again in July 1993 to pave the way for negotiations over a new social and economic pact to commence in the autumn. González, who met separately with employers' leaders, pledged to make job creation the major plank of a new 2- to 3-year agreement and sought wage restraint from the unions and a reinvestment of profits from the employers as crucial

Table 7.3 *Spanish trade-union membership (20 per cent), late 1980s*

Trade union	No. of members	% total membership
Workers' Commissions	730,000	42.0
UGT	692,000	39.9
Workers' Syndical Union (USO)	205,000	11.8
Basque TU (ELA/STV)	58,000	3.4
Other/Regional TUs	53,000	2.9

Source: *Cambio 16*

elements of such a pact. The trade unions, on the other hand, sought the government's continued commitment to a new more liberal strike law as a key bargaining counter in negotiations. The fact that both sides of industry were again in discussion with the government after years of hostility suggested that harsh economic realities were finally forging renewed consensus.

Trade-union membership

The unreliable figures provided by the unions themselves make membership levels difficult to estimate, although independent observers believe that membership in recent years has fallen away from that of the late 1970s, when it may have reached a maximum of 30 per cent of the working population. The current level is unlikely to be much higher than 20 per cent, the level attained in 1981, and the lowest in Western Europe.

A May 1989 article in the Spanish magazine *Cambio 16* (Table 7.3) estimated membership at 17 per cent, but what is certain is that existing trade unions are ill-organized and inefficient. Poor collection procedures mean that between 50 per cent and 70 per cent of total membership dues are probably not collected. Strike funds are minimal, so that extended strikes are only possible in small companies or those areas where the local population identifies closely with the demands of the workforce.

New initiatives

The UGT estimates that within a few years half its funds will derive from the profits of a new holding company it is establishing, UGTSA. The holding company will be led by a new trade-union bank; by a house-building corporation, PSV, which will promote cooperative ventures; and by an insurance company, UNIAL.

These three companies will form the basis of the holding company, as the UGT attempts to achieve financial autonomy, distancing itself from the Socialist party, and setting out to become a huge service trade union like its counterparts elsewhere in Western Europe. UNIAL, with forty-six offices projected throughout Spain, and with the use of UGT offices, has ambitions to attract business beyond the UGT membership itself. UGT points out that in Sweden, for instance, one person in two invests in a trade-union insurance company, while in Austria a union company is market leader in the sector.

Conclusion

The Spanish trade unions are still in the early years of their renascent emergence from the Franco period. They have achieved an importance and a role in Spanish public life out of all proportion to their membership levels, and their leaders are household names. They have a responsibility that is paradoxically also their greatest problem, since the basis of their power – membership and organizational structure – is still fragile. By engaging in consensus politics up to the end of 1986, the unions played a vital role in Spain's economic revolution. When they sat down again with the Prime Minister on 5 July 1993, after years of confrontation, they once again faced the opportunity to assist in Spain's emergence from recession and high unemployment. The question was whether the unions would allow the biggest stumbling block to a new social and economic pact desperately required by Spain, namely the Government's desire to introduce greater flexibility into the labour market, to divert them from their wider responsibilities to the workforce and the country.

8 Business and employers' organizations

Introduction

The Franco era left a climate of deep suspicions among many employees about employers and employers' organizations. The vertical syndicate system under Franco effectively gave all power to employers and none to the workforce. Only employers were represented at the upper levels of government. The emergence of political pluralism and free democratic debate from the embers of the Francoist system gave rise to political parties and trade unions that were able to articulate the demands of their supporters successfully. It was less clear or certain in 1980 how or whether Spanish employers could find organizations and leaders to represent their views amid the maelstrom of rhetoric issuing from every section of Spanish society.

Background

Spain has not enjoyed a long tradition of employers' organizations, although some regional organizations did exist before 1975, especially in Catalonia, the first region of Spain to be developed industrially. However, Article 7 of the constitution recognized the significance of employers' organizations and their right to defend and promote the interests of their members. They are required by the constitution to have a democratic structure and operation, and to be properly registered. Article 37 also alludes to their role in the representation of employers in the collective bargaining process and Article 131 implicity allocates them a role in the economic planning of the country.

Since 1978, many organizations at national, regional, local and sectorial level have been formed. Under the Franco regime, employers, like employees, compulsorily formed part of the vertical syndicate system, organized by sectors of industry. Many of the current employers' organizations have evolved out of the sectorial links created at that time.

The CEOE

The main employers' confederation in Spain is the **Confederación Española de Organizaciones Empresariales** (Spanish Confederation of Employers' Organizations or CEOE), which was formed in 1977 to provide an umbrella organization for numerous firms of all sizes. The CEOE claims to have 1.3 million members, which control 75 per cent of all jobs in Spain in the private sector. It must be remembered of course that 90 per cent of firms employ fewer than 500 workers, and there is therefore potential for a large number of members of employers' organizations.

The CEOE encompasses firms and affiliated employers' associations, especially the small and medium-sized firms that belong to the **Confederación Española de Pequeñas y Medianas Empresas** (Spanish Confederation of Small- and Medium-Sized Firms or CEPYME). As Donaghy and Newton point out in *Spain: A Guide to Political and Economic Institutions*, the need for the establishment of the CEOE was highlighted by the initiation of a consensual approach to economic and labour problems in 1977, which culminated in the signing of the Moncloa Pacts on the economy, an agreement between the main political parties and emergent trade unions to take necessary *ad hoc* economic and fiscal measures. The fact that the employers were not represented in the Moncloa Pacts was a major spur to the formation of CEOE as an umbrella organization. Since 1977, CEOE has grown into an effective body incorporating some 165 individual employers' organizations, of which forty-nine are intersectorial and region-based and the remainder are sectorial, representing activities such as banking, iron and steel, advertising and construction, organized on a national or regional basis (see Table 8.1).

CEPYME, the association for small- and medium-sized firms, itself a national and regional organization, was integrated into the CEOE in 1980. However, it still preserves special autonomous status within the larger grouping and appeared as a separate signatory to the social and economic pacts made with government and the unions (see Chapter 7, pp. 69–71).

The principal policy-making body of the CEOE is the general assembly, which comprises 600 delegates elected by the 165 employers' organizations that form the confederation. The general assembly elects the chairman and a board of management every 3 years, and this board appoints an executive committee of twenty-four members. The CEOE maintains a number of committees and sub-committees, which report

Table 8.1 *Examples of membership of CEOE (Spanish Employers' Confederation)*

Ambit	Title	Sector
National	Confederación Española de Pequeñas y Medianas Empresas (CEPYME)	Small- and medium-sized firms
	Confederación Española de Mujeres Empresarias (CEME)	Employers of women
Regional	Confederación de Empresarios de Andalucía (CEA)	Andalusia
	Fomento del Trabajo Nacional	Catalonia
Sectorial	Asociación Empresarial de Agencias de Viajes (AEDAVE)	Travel agencies
	Asociación Española de Banca (AEB)	Banks
	Asociación Empresarial de Publicidad Exterior (AEPE)	Advertising
	Asociación Nacional de Fabricantes de Automóviles (ANFAC)	Car manufacture
	Asociación de Navieros Españoles (ANAVE)	Shipbuilding
	Confederación Empresarial de Metal (CONFEMETAL)	Iron and steel
	Confederación Nacional de la Construcción (CNC)	Construction

Source: Donaghy and Newton, *Spain: A Guide to Political and Economic Institutions*

to the board of management and to a full-time secretariat. The latter services the committees and helps them research and report on economic, labour and international matters of concern. The CEOE is funded in two main ways: first, by membership fees, which constitute the bulk of the confederation's income; and second, by direct subsidy from the government, in recognition of the CEOE's special role in Spain. The latter funding parallels subsidies received by the trade unions and political parties from the central exchequer.

The CEOE's primary role is to act as the main representative organization for the employers. This role has been successfully secured at the cost of two rival national bodies – the **Confederacíon General de las Pequeñas y Medianas Empresas del Estado Español** (General Confederation of Small- and Medium-Sized Firms of Spain or COPYME), and the **Unión de la Pequeña y Mediana Empresa** (Union of Small- and Medium-Sized Firms or UNIPYME). Both COPYME and UNIPYME have had to take a back seat as the CEOE, increasingly combative and assertive, has assumed an important public profile since the mid-1980s, taking advantage of the unions' weakness through lack of funds, lack of unity (with notable exceptions such as the 1988 general strike) and the employment situation.

The CEOE does not negotiate collective agreements on behalf of employers, a task that is left to individual associations, usually at regional, local or sectorial level, but it does negotiate on pay terms and working conditions at a national level. The CEOE also represents employers on official bodies in which provision is made for employer and worker participation, such as the social security institutions INSS, INSERSO and INSALUD. In addition, the CEOE provides advisory, consultative and training facilities for its members and represents employers at an international level, for example *vis-à-vis* the International Labour Organization (ILO). The CEOE has also established an office in Brussels, which monitors EC developments on behalf of Spanish employers.

The CEOE and wage negotiations

After collaborating in a number of social and economic pacts with the trade unions and/or government up to 1986, the CEOE adopted a more intransigent attitude in the late 1980s, articulating clear and uncompromising demands to government, especially the demand for greater flexibility in employment, which the trade unions were not prepared to entertain. The trade-unions' impasse with the González government (see pp. 72–75) left the CEOE in an intermediate position but one decidedly nearer the viewpoint of the government than that of the unions. The late 1980s and early 1990s witnessed tacit although muted support from the CEOE for a central government that was attempting to introduce greater flexibility and mobility in the labour market as a means of improving Spain's international competitiveness and ameliorating the unemployment position. Such was the hostility between trade unions and government, however, that the prospect of a further social and economic accord was at no time realistic during the 1987 to 1993 period.

González's pledge, following his re-election as head of a minority government in June 1993, to enter into dialogue with all representative sectors of Spanish society, however, created a different climate in Spain. Even before his inauguration as Prime Minister González sat down with trade-union leaders and with José María Cuevas, the CEOE chairman, in July 1993, to map out future negotiations, with a new social and economic pact at the top of the political agenda. The CEOE had already drawn up its shopping list of requirements from a new agreement. The main demands were as follows:

- New rules for negotiating colllective agreements.
- National criteria for fixing wage levels.
- Strong government action to counter social security fraud.
- Improvements in managing the social security and benefit payments.
- Greater flexibility in employment conditions and changes in employer/employee contracts.
- New machinery for resolving industrial disputes.

Cuevas emphasized that the CEOE were more interested in giving employers greater control over workforce contracts and conditions of employment than in wage negotiations alone. González for his part promised Cuevas and trade-union leaders that both sides of industry would be fully consulted in the run-up to the presentation of the government budget for 1994 in the autumn of 1993. After years of non-existent dialogue between government, employers and unions, Spain faced the real prospect of progress toward another social and economic accord, which most commentators saw as an essential prerequisite of the country's attempts to climb out of recession.

Chambers of commerce

The **cámaras de comercio** (chambers of commerce) are classed by Article 52 of the constitution as professional organizations, i.e. organizations other than employers' organizations, unions or professional associations, which exist to defend their members' economic interests. As with the CEOE, the constitution requires that chambers of commerce must be democratic and regulated by law.

The Spanish chambers of commerce have a long tradition, dating back to the nineteenth century. They perform a similar role to equivalent bodies in other EC countries in that they provide a range of services to firms and individuals they represent; these include economic and financial advice, research and information, help in export promotion, representation abroad, trade missions and documentation, and legal services. The chambers of commerce also advise central, regional and local government on issues pertaining to business and commerce. As official bodies ultimately responsible to the Ministry of Economy and Finance, their role could be said to be larger than that enjoyed by their counterparts in EC partner states. The major discernible difference is that membership of a chamber of commerce in Spain is not voluntary. All those engaged in the activities covered by the chamber are automatically members, whether as individual traders or as firms. The fees they pay come in the form of a 2 per cent tax surcharge on normal payments, which the chamber is responsible for collecting. The internal organization of the chambers of commerce parallels that of other countries in that a general plenary meeting of elected delegates decides overall policy, and a smaller executive committee takes management decisions through the year. All the chambers of commerce, which are located in Spain's major cities with smaller chambers at provincial level, are members of an umbrella organization located in Madrid, the National Council of Chambers of Commerce, which co-ordinates and disseminates information nationwide and represents the chambers nationally and internationally.

The chairman of the National Council, Guillermo de la Dehesa, received much publicity in 1992 for his views on the role of the chambers in post-1992 Europe. His vision was that the chambers, in addition to their usual role, must work more closely with chambers in other EC countries. The main aims and objectives of the chambers were to provide information and training, to give logistical help to firms, and to guide firms on the necessity of adaptation. These were not merely theoretical aims, however, and the Spanish chambers began to take a more hands-on and pro-active role in the early 1990s by producing a series of practical initiatives under the heading of Plans of Action of the Chambers. The first of this was an export promotion plan with four main objectives: to concentrate on the export performance of small- and medium-sized companies; to increase the number of firms exporting; to co-ordinate exporting endeavours; and to strengthen the chambers' presence and impact abroad.

Business fairs

One of the major tasks of the chambers of commerce is the organization of business fairs in Spain, a task the chambers normally share with regional and local government. The number and the extent of business fairs have increased very dramatically in the 1980s. In 1979, only forty-one fairs were held in Spain, but this number had increased to 214 by 1990. Their proliferation has also assisted the construction industry as new permanent and temporary sites are constructed. It is estimated that, in 1990, business fairs generated 1,000 permanent jobs and 7,000 temporary jobs with an average duration of 20 days.

Not only are the fairs good business, but they are crucial to elevating Spain's international business profile. The 1-week International Fashion Fair in Madrid in 1989 generated almost 4 million pesetas in income and attracted 2 million visitors. Spain's fashion industry now has seventeen delegations working abroad, and many of them work with foreign chambers of commerce. The international business fair market is still growing rapidly in Spain; 116 major international fairs were held in Spain in 1992, with more planned for 1993. The most popular venues were Madrid

Table 8.2 *Examples of professional associations*

Title of association	Profession
Colegio Oficial de Arquitectos	Architects
Instituto de Censores Jurados de Cuentas de España	Auditors
Colegio Oficial de Ingenieros de Construcción	Construction engineers
Colegio de Médicos	Doctors
Colegio de Economistas	Economists
Colegio de Abogados	Lawyers
Colegio Oficial de Físicos	Physicists
Colegio Oficial de Agentes de Cambio y Bolsa	Stockbrokers and exchange dealers

Source: *Anuario El País*

(twenty-nine fairs), Valencia (twenty-seven) and Barcelona (twenty-one), and the most active sector was the consumer goods industry.

Other professional associations

The 1978 constitution legitimized the existence of **colegios profesionales** (professional associations), which in many cases, unlike free trade unions, were allowed to continue under Franco. The associations are important because any individual wishing to exercise a particular profession is obliged to belong to the appropriate branch of the relevant association. The professional associations themselves must govern their operations in accordance with statutes approved by the particular government ministry to which their profession pertains. For example, the **Colegio de Médicos** (Doctors' association) is ultimately responsible to the Ministry of Health and the **Colegio de abogados** (lawyers' association) to the Ministry of Justice. Table 8.2 provides examples of some of the better-known professional associations.

The major associations have regional offices as well as national headquarters. Although there are varying types of internal organization, each association will normally have a **consejo general** (general council) and a **presidente** (chairman). As well as providing information and support services for members, the associations also have a role in advising government, at national, regional, or local level, on matters pertaining to their profession. By maintaining a register of members, they are able to safeguard professional standards and can strike off the register any member found to be deficient in his exercise of the profession.

Conclusion

The 1980s saw the emergence of employers' organizations as major play-ers in economic and political decision-making in Spain. Whereas the Spanish Employers' Confederation, the CEOE, was unknown outside its member organizations in 1980, by the end of the decade, the CEOE and its chairman had the ear of government and commanded the attention of the media in a way comparable to that of the Confederation of British Industry in the UK. As the CEOE's chairman, José María Cuevas, called for government to take additional measures to help business converge with Europe, the chambers of commerce were setting the pace by assist-ing Spanish companies to export and by providing foreign investors with guidance on opportunities in Spain. Spanish employers, both small and large, could feel confident that their interests would be properly articu-lated in any new social and economic pact struck with government and the trade unions.

9 Business, education, training and development

Introduction

In evaluating the contribution made to the Spanish business culture by education, training and development, it must be realized that Spain is starting in this area from a very low base. The decades of Francoism held back educational reforms, and it was only in 1970 that an education reform act introduced the educational structure still largely in place today. The act, however, in revolutionizing schooling, did not solve many of its attendant problems. Hence, a major plank of the first Socialist government's legislative programme in the 1980s was further educational reform, to be effected by two new laws, the 1983 LRU (University Reform Law) and the 1985 LODE (Organic Law on the Right to Education), designed to democratize and modernize the school and university system. In 1990, the most far-reaching of all Spanish educational reforms was introduced, the LOGSE (Organic Law on the General Organization of the Education System). This law seeks to widen nursery provision, to make secondary schooling 'comprehensive', and to improve technical education.

The democratic transition inherited from Franco one of the least educated or trained workforces in the Western world. The impact of 1970 education legislation was felt, however, as the percentage of unskilled workers fell from 46 per cent in 1963 to 33 per cent in 1976. The increase in skilled workers was particularly noticeable in administrative jobs, which constituted 12 per cent of wage-earners in 1963 but increased to 19 per cent by 1976. The standard of education changed also, so that, in the 1970s, education among workers to secondary school level became common for the first time, whereas previously the majority of workers had only reached primary level, if that. In 1964, only 5 per cent of the active population had secondary education. By 1980, it was almost 25 per cent.

The prioritization of educational reform by successive post-Franco governments has met with the approbation of the OECD. But it may be a decade or more before it is possible to assess the effects of the latest law on academic standards and the quality of technical training and business management.

The other great sea-change in education since the restoration of democracy has brought about greater devolution and democratization in the system. The Spanish education system has historically resembled the French rather than the British model, with everything under the centralized control of the Ministry of Education in Madrid. In the mid-1990s, central government still maintains a number of responsibilities over education, the most important of which are as follows:

- Overall legislation and planning.
- Regulation and validation of certificates and degrees.
- Organization of the system's different levels and of minimum subject matter.
- Establishment of minimum conditions with which educational institutions must comply.

The remaining responsibilities in the field of education have been transferred to the regional governments, which administer the educational system within their region. In particular, the regions have special responsibilities for the autonomous universities which have their own languages – in Catalonia, Galicia and the Basque Country. The universities as a whole now have widespread autonomous powers after centuries of control from Madrid and have moved much closer to the Anglo-Saxon model, although the differences still outweigh the similarities.

The LODE established **consejos escolares** (school councils) to channel the participation of society in management of schools. These councils, which may be compared to governing bodies or boards in the UK, are made up of teacher, student and parent representatives, and, in the case of private schools, the owners as well. State schools have political representation also. The school councils' main functions, somewhat less than the powers of UK schools under devolved local management, are as follows:

- To elect the principal.
- To approve and apply internal regulations.
- To establish an annual programme of activities.
- To approve and supervise the budget.
- To apply student admission requirements.
- To intervene in the hiring and firing of teachers in the case of private schools.

Primary and secondary education

Pre-school education in Spain is divided into play-schools (0–3 years of age) and nursery schools (4–5 years). The play-schools are very diverse in character; many are part of day-care centres and belong to businesses, city councils, foundations or are run on private initiative. Enrolment at this age is minimal, little more than 10 per cent. Nursery education, however, has made tremendous strides in recent years, with approximately 96 per cent of 4- and 5-year-olds attending schools often located within state or privately owned primary schools. Despite greater take-up, the total number of pupils in pre-school education has fallen, as a result of the decrease in the birthrate, from 1.1 million in 1985 to less than 1 million in 1992.

For their primary schooling, all pupils between the ages of 6 and 14 go to state or private schools, to study the compulsory EGB (basic general education course). Pupils study a range of compulsory and optional subjects, with a compulsory modern language – English has rapidly replaced French in recent years. At the age of 14 the more academically able go on to study for a 2-year **Bachillerato** while for others a course of vocational training known as **Formación Profesional** (FP) is available. The separation at 14 has caused innumerable problems, since parents have tended to keep their children in the academic lane by having them repeat years rather than allowing them to proceed along the less prestigious FP route. FP diplomas have also been slow to gain acceptance from Spanish employers.

The new 1990 LOGSE law will eventually extend the period of obligatory education to the age of 16, thus avoiding premature specialization in a particular area of the curriculum.

Access to the universities is generally via the **COU** (university orientation course), a 1-year pre-university course, with three compulsory subjects (Spanish language and literature, a foreign language and mathematics) and three optional subjects. In recent years, other 'selectivity' exams have provided a route to higher education, which saw a rapid expansion in the 1970s and 1980s to the level of 960,000 university students in the academic year 1991–2 (compared with 383,000 in 1975).

Private education has traditionally been very important at pre-university level, and has been tied closely to the Catholic Church. During the 1991–2 school year it was estimated that the following proportion of pupils were registered at private schools: 35 per cent of pre-school age, 35 per cent of primary, and 34 per cent on technical training courses. Only 3 per cent attended private universities. Approximately one-third of all non-university education is private, with the Catholic Church controlling approximately 20 per cent of the whole educational system.

Until quite recently, the typical clientèle of private education comprised the middle and upper classes, who could afford it, while state education was predominantly geared to the lower classes. In the 1980s, legislation radically altered this trend, however, not by eliminating private education but by establishing totally free education in the state sector and by exercising academic quality controls over both the state and private sector. Whereas previously there was little or no control over much of the curriculum in private schools, now these schools, if they wish to continue receiving state subsidies, must enter into an agreement with the state that means offering the same curriculum as state schools. The effects of these and more recent legislative changes are still being felt, but first signs indicate a definite improvement in standards in both state and private schools.

Universities

The spectacular rise in student numbers has caused chaos in a university system originally designed to accommodate only a tenth of the current student population. It has added to the problem of 'massification', i.e. the anonymous, impersonal, distant and bureaucratic treatment of students by institutions living, until recently, in the last century. The González government has, in the University Reform Law, attempted to update the universities, by placing tighter limits on the numbers admitted, in order to improve academic standards, by reorganizing university departments along Anglo-Saxon lines, and by reducing the bureaucracy that was strangling the system. (For instance, the Law reduced the forty-five categories of university teachers to four!) Naturally, the restrictions on numbers generated the most vociferous public protests and demonstrations.

Currently, there are thirty-nine universities in Spain, including four private, church-owned universities, the consequence of the 1953 concordat between the state and the Catholic Church. These four universities suffer the least from 'massification'. The biggest universities in Spain are the Complutense in Madrid, Barcelona Central, Santiago de Compostela and Valencia. In all of them there is a space crisis, with Salamanca's half a square metre per student not untypical. The top universities, in terms of research expertise, are Complutense and Barcelona Central. However, the universities suffer from a lack of teaching staff with expertise in business and management studies, and in technology.

Spain also has its UNED (National University for Distance Learning) – the equivalent of the United Kingdom's Open University – which was inaugurated in 1972. It has been consistently underfunded ever since, however, so that numbers have only grown relatively slowly from 40,000 in 1984 to 87,000 in 1991.

Government plans for universities

In 1989–90, the Spanish government, looking beyond 1992, announced a further overhaul of the university system. The main components of the new plan were as follows:

- The criteria of productivity is to be applied in determining the salaries of university lecturers, with top rates for academic high-fliers.
- Students, for the first time in Spain, will be able to study at any university rather than at the nearest.
- A ranking list of universities is to be drawn up to encourage more competition in the sector.
- New, more relevant, and shorter degree courses are to be phased in, e.g. eighty new (mostly 3-year) degrees were introduced in 1989–90, and more followed in subsequent years.
- Spain's first non-religious private university is to be established, specializing in law and economics (the Escuela Libre de Derecho y Economía).
- New university campuses are to be founded in Madrid and Barcelona.
- The Ministry of Education is to create a new system of university grants. Until now grants have been few and difficult to obtain.

Opposition from university staff trade unions to some of these measures did not prevent their full implementation.

New private universities

A bill presented in the Spanish parliament in 1990 facilitated the creation of new private universities in Spain. A number of projects have been under examination, including two in Madrid and one each in Barcelona and Valencia. The Catholic Church, owners of private schools and a number of major companies, have all expressed interest in the idea.

While the Private University of Madrid, run by private school proprietors, is expected to be first to open, with 12,000 students on two campuses, the most innovative aspect of the venture is the interest being shown by Spanish companies. The banks, BNP and Banco Central Hispanoamericano, Repsol (the petrol giant), and El Aguila (brewers) all want to be involved, but perhaps the most unusual application is that of the oil company Petromed, which is pursuing its interest in a private university jointly with Mercedes-Benz under the aegis of the EC ERASMUS initiative.

Table 9.1   *Spanish education: input and output indicators (1975 and 1985)*

	1975	1985
Pre-university education		
Number of pupils (thousands)	7,517	8,696
State schools	4,340	5,593
Pre-primary	920	1,127
Compulsory	5,473	5,594
Post-compulsory (FP)	305	737
Post-compulsory (general)	818	1,238
Number of teachers in state schools (thousands)	156	271
Higher education		
Students (thousands)	557	822

Source: OECD

Technical training

While university student numbers have grown in recent years, so also have pupils studying vocational training under the Formación Profesional (FP) banner. Numbers have doubled between 1975 and 1991. In the same period, the enrolment rate in education increased by two-thirds while the number of students in higher education as a share of the total population rose by 50 per cent.

A growing mismatch between employer demand and supply of labour at all levels has been increasingly noticeable since the 1980s. Industry has been experiencing longer delays in filling vacancies. A recent survey by the Ministry of Labour demonstrated that FP is not providing the skills and qualifications firms need. Hence, with government support, new professional training programmes have been initiated in order to improve the quality of labour supply, especially in sectors with a skilled labour shortage.

Numbers of students and teachers are listed in Table 9.1.

Management training

Business executives in Spain are very well paid in comparison with their EC counterparts and generally more so the higher up they go. The business revolution of the 1980s was accompanied by an explosion of interest among young people in pursuing a business career. As a result, many thousands of bright young executives are streaming out of the business schools and the universities to become sharp managers.

Spanish business schools have been proliferating since the late 1980s in an attempt to meet spiralling demand. The Ministry of Labour estimates, however, that Spanish firms require a minimum of 30,000 executives per year trained in business and management studies. Spanish business schools in fact are only producing 11,000 per year and not all of these are trained to a sufficiently high level.

The first MBAs appeared in Spanish business schools in the mid-1960s, and the schools themselves are flourishing, but the failure to apply strict criteria on the qualifications awarded has meant that any educational institution can appropriate the title 'Masters' and apply it to virtually any course of any standard or duration. Thus, many business schools and even the in-house training agencies of the Cajas de ahorros have been attaching the 'Masters' label to courses on an indiscriminate and arbitrary basis. Another problem is that in Spain, unlike the USA, for example, no ranking list of business schools is produced.

Despite the problems, demand in the marketplace is very high indeed, with Spain's top business school **Instituto de Estudios Superiores de Empresa** (IESI), in Navarra, regularly attracting in excess of 2,000 applications for its 200 MBA places, and with even the less prestigious schools receiving at least four or five applications per place. One of Spain's leading business magazines, *España Económica*, suggested recently that the market could probably absorb ten times the number of places currently available.

By general consent, the top business schools in Spain of a standard comparable with those of other EC countries are IESI, **Escuela Superior de Administración y Dirección de Empresas** (ESADE) in Barcelona, and the **Instituto de Empresas** in Madrid. New schools are opening up, though, to supply market demand, e.g. the new Madrid Business School. IESI estimates that each student graduating with a qualification receives an average of three job offers, while other schools claim this can rise to eight per student. The business schools of Madrid and Barcelona account for about 80 per cent of student intake amid ferocious competition for the best students.

An indication of rising standards and the growing esteem in which the top Spanish business schools are held is the increase in US, Canadian and other European students on MBA courses in Spain. The US magazine *Fortune*, in its ranking of the top five business schools in Europe put IESI (which incidentally introduced the oldest MBA in Europe, in 1964, in conjunction with Harvard) in fifth place behind INSEAD (Fontainebleau), London Business School, IMEDE (Lausanne) and IMI (Geneva). IESI's ranking is undoubtedly due to its rigorous training programme for would-be lecturers, who spend 3 or 4 years in a top US business school such as Harvard before returning to lecture in Spain.

Research and development

In February 1988, the government approved a National Plan for Scientific Research and Technological development. The Plan, which came into operation in the autumn of 1988, aims to raise the scientific and techno-logical base, especially in terms of research, in higher education and in companies. The base, historically, has been very low, with research grants, which were first awarded in 1968, having little or no relevance to the world of business.

For many years R & D has constituted only about 0.4 per cent of GDP, although this level doubled in the second half of the 1980s, increasing from 0.48 per cent GDP in 1984 to 0.85 per cent GDP in 1990 (equivalent to 300,000 million pesetas). The Plan aimed to raise the level further to 1.2 per cent of GDP by 1992, a substantial increase, although this must be set against the almost 3 per cent of GDP devoted to R & D in Germany.

A prime aim of the Plan is to train greater numbers of personnel up to masters' and doctorate level in order better to face the challenge of post-1992 Europe. A massive investment in training in priority areas includes provision for sending more Spaniards abroad for training. Over 20 per cent of the national plan's budget is allocated to the training of researchers. In 1980, there were the equivalent of 14,000 researchers working full-time in Spain; by 1991, this figure had doubled, with further expansion planned. Approximately 66 per cent of those engaged in re-search in Spain are connected with the universities and other public institutions, with 34 per cent found in private and state-owned industry. This ratio compares poorly with those of other EC partners (an average of 50 : 50) but is gradually balancing out as immense educational efforts are made to increase the 9,000 scholarship research students by prioritizing research areas of potential interest to industry.

Research centres have in the past dominated the research climate and the more important of these, such as the multidisciplinary CSIC (Council for Scientific Research) and the National Institute of Aerospace Technol-ogy have in recent years made greater efforts to bridge the gap to indus-try. Such moves are consistent with the National Plan, which aspires to improving the research base in industry, for R & D has hitherto virtually been ignored in that field. The Plan envisages the establishment of struc-tures to improve the integration of scientific research with technological knowhow and industrial experience, i.e. the plan proposes to link the universities, government research councils and Spanish companies. A crucial element in this is the creation of a national network, OTRI (**Office for Relay of Research Results**), which will co-ordinate research projects and findings in all of Spain's universities and will eventually access these to Spanish industry. The Plan also seeks to boost the participation of Spanish firms and universities in various EC programmes, such as EUREKA and the European Space Agency.

Spanish companies are reacting positively to the challenge of updating technology in order to boost competitiveness at home and abroad. In the period 1970–87, Spanish firms quadrupled their R & D budgets (at constant values), the rise being one of the most dramatic in the OECD. State-owned industries, such as INI, Telefónica and RENFE, have led the way in the defence, aeronautics and communications fields, while in the private sector, the most dynamic industries in terms of R & D investment have been pharmaceutical and chemical products, electronics and information technology, and transportation equipment.

In addition to central government and industry initiatives, a number of regional governments also began to award research grants in the late 1980s. The sum total of all these efforts has helped to raise the international profile of Spanish researchers, as evidenced in the *Science Citation Index*, which recorded a 13 per cent growth in Spanish publications in the world's top scientific journals between 1987 and 1988. Initial results are therefore encouraging, but the 1988 experience also indicated that demand for research grants to study abroad in certain vital areas is woefully inferior to the country's requirements. Less than twenty applications apiece were received in the areas of agrarian research, marine research, and information technology, while some areas such as robotics attracted no applicants at all.

Recognizing the problem, the Education Minister, in early 1990, committed an additional 11,000 million pesetas to scholarships and funding for training research students, an enormous boost to the ministry's campaign to increase the number and quality of researchers and scientists. Also in 1992, the National R & D Plan entered its second phase (1992–5), to continue the groundwork carried out in the earlier stage. The second phase acknowledged that Spain's R & D base was still much worse than those of other countries, with R & D in 1990 accounting for less than 1 per cent of GDP in Spain compared with 1.25 per cent in Italy, 2.3 per cent in the UK and France, 2.9 per cent in Germany, and 3 per cent in Japan and the United States. The Plan envisaged much greater research co-operation outside the EC as well as within it. Thus, in the early 1990s, a number of research and scientific agreements were signed with central and eastern European countries, and a massive new R & D investment was destined for Latin America through AECI (the Spanish Agency for International Co-operation).

Conclusion

Spain has invested heavily in education training and development since the early 1990s in an effort to catch up with other countries (up until 1980

Spain was still considered a 'developing' country by the IMF and the World Bank). The amount spent on education increased 145 per cent between 1985 and 1991 alone, while educational opportunity was placed at the top of the government's agenda: the student grant budget increased by 1,000 per cent in the 1980s. Financial investment was accompanied by a radical overhaul of the education system at all levels. It is too early to assess the full impact of all these changes but it is already possible to assert with some confidence that Spain's business confraternity can only benefit from the expected improvements in academic, vocational and research standards. In particular, a growing Europeanization of Spanish education is discernible as rising numbers of Spanish students and educational institutions benefit from EC exchange and mobility programmes.

10   Business and the environment

Introduction

The business culture in Spain is only just beginning to be aware of environmental issues, which are relatively new on the political and business agenda and occupy the nation's attention far less than in most other EC countries. Thus, while ecology groups and 'green' parties emerged in Spain in the 1980s, they have not hitherto achieved the public profile or the electoral support seen elsewhere. In the general elections of 1989 and 1993, the environment was one of the lesser campaign issues, and only one party, the opposition Popular Party, advocated the creation of a government ministry of the environment to bring Spain into line with her European partners. Ironically, Spain receives most aid from Brussels under the EC cohesion fund, which seeks to assist poorer EC nations to improve their environment and their infrastructure.

The rapid changes of the past 30 years, however, have created in Spain a massive environmental problem, the scale of which Spaniards are finally appreciating when, for instance, the air pollution in towns like Madrid makes it virtually impossible to breathe on occasions or when the polluted nature of Spain's Mediterranean beaches and coastal towns attracts the unwelcome attention of the foreign media (as happened in the summer of 1989 when the resort of Salou, south of Barcelona, was condemned by the British popular press). The results of an industrialization process that brought a massive exodus from the countryside to the towns in the 1960s, and the uncontrolled development of manufacturing industry, were accompanied by all the depredations that mass tourism and its service industries brought to Spain's coastlines. The 1980s perceived the problem; the 1990s have barely begun to address it.

Responsibility for the environment

Central government promulgates environmental legislation while the regions may pass supplementary regulations. Only in 1972 did Spain approve its first legislation on the environment and establish a public body to co-ordinate environmental policy, known as the **Comisión Interministerial del Medio Ambiente** (Inter-ministerial Committee for the Environment or CIMA), responsible to the **Ministerio de Obras Públicas y Urbanismo** (Ministry for Public Works and Town-planning). CIMA's decisions, however, were not legally binding and its limited scope prevented it from achieving many objectives. Environmental issues emerged under different government ministries – industry, agriculture, health, transport, etc. – but the lack of a single government department responsible for environmental affairs was an obvious impediment to rapid address of the problem.

Only in 1992 did Spain finally appoint an Environment Minister, José Borell, but the fact that he is also Minister for Transport and Public Works, a department that is the worst offender against EC green laws, justifies criticism that he is both 'gamekeeper and poacher'! Spain's ability to improve environmental standards to EC norms is still therefore constrained by the absence of an administrative unit for environmental policy. There is still no single body for centralizing and co-ordinating environmental policy, and, above all, none with weight and influence at ministry level to develop more 'ecological' policies for the ministries. Presently, the policies and measures concerning wildlife are the responsibility of ICONA (Institute for Nature Conservation), which comes under the Ministry of Agriculture, Fisheries and Food. The policies and measures for environmental policy in general are the responsibility of the Head Office for the Environment, which comes under the Ministry of Transport and Public Works. These two organizations often do not work in a co-ordinated way, or co-operate.

Similarly, there is in practice no co-ordination between regional governments, which can legislate on different matters in autonomous and independent ways that are sometimes contradictory. At regional level, notably in Andalusia and Asturias, some attempts have been made to establish **Agencias de Medio Ambiente** (environmental agencies) but these have not so far met with conspicuous success. The lack of a single body at central government level and the lack of regional co-ordination both hinder practical compliance with EC regulations.

Another important problem for implementation of EC legislation is the absence of an efficient monitoring and inspection system. Although attempts are being made to remedy this situation, Spain still does not have any inspectorate for environmental matters, except for approximately 100 foresters who work only on the conservation of wildlife in protected areas. Recently, the Spanish Civil Guard (Spanish Military Institution) was granted responsibility for environmental monitoring and inspection. This project is already in the formulation stage, and without any doubt if it continues successfully it will be an important step in the matter of practical compliance.

Table 10.1 *Spanish emissions of atmospheric pollutants by industry (1980)*

Sector	Particulates (1,000 tonnes)	Sulphur dioxide (1,000 tonnes)	Nitrogen oxides (1,000 tonnes)
Power stations	341	1,610	186
Oil refineries	–	130	17
Iron and steel works	214	178	–
Cement works	268	50	11
Sulphuric acid plants	–	38	6
Paper mills	21	44	8

Source: European Commission

Since the scale of Spain's environment problem far outweighs the remedial measures taken hitherto, the major environmental issues the political and the business community must face in the 1990s are summarized below. Where appropriate, the response to date of government and business is outlined.

Air and noise pollution

Legislation from 1972 governs the prevention, monitoring and correction of air pollution, and establishes acceptable emission levels. Special provisions were made for the worst affected areas, mainly the areas with the highest concentration of heavy industry – Bilbao, Madrid, Avilés, Huelva, Cartagena – and the first anti-air pollution campaigns were launched with government grants. The worst offenders in terms of industrial air pollution are power stations, oil refineries, iron and steel works and cement works. See Table 10.1.

In the late 1980s, government and industry began to work together to counter air pollution. As well as grants and tax concessions to firms, government has also made available to firms in high-pollution areas special subsidies for up to 30 per cent of the total cost of installing anti-pollution equipment. In addition, in 1985, the first legislation was passed to improve vehicular air pollution, when the lead content of petrol was reduced from 0.6g/L to 0.44g/L, in line with EC regulations.

Spain's entry into the EC in 1986 necessitated considerable efforts to adapt and apply community rules on air pollution. In 1986 and 1987, legislation established new norms for air quality with regard to pollution by sulphur dioxide and particles, and by nitric acid and lead. This has contributed to improving air quality in the big cities by bringing about considerable reductions in emissions from heating installations, industry and automobiles. The EC directive concerning reduction of sulphur dioxide and nitric oxide emissions from large combustion plants is currently being implemented in three phases up to 2003.

In terms of noise pollution, Spanish legislation is fragmentary, and, only in the early 1990s, did central government introduce legislation to fix maximum permitted noise levels for the whole country and to establish maximum levels for noise emissions from equipment and machinery. A number of surveys carried out between 1978 and 1986 had shown that noise was one of the main problems of the urban environment. The surveys found that the situation was serious or very serious in 48 per cent of towns with populations of between 100,000 and 500,000, while 67 per cent of towns with over 500,000 inhabitants reported an extremely serious situation. Spain is, in addition, one of the OECD countries most exposed to vehicle traffic noise. While awaiting national legislation, a number of local authorities have passed noise ordinances in the past decade, while some large towns sensitive to the problem of noise pollution – notably Madrid, Barcelona, and Zaragoza – have begun to take measures to reduce noise levels.

According to available data, the acidification of the environment (acid rain) does not have the importance in Spain that it does in other countries of central Europe. Rainfall and acid residues are considerably lower than the European average, and a large part of the national territory has a calcareous composition, making it less sensitive to this problem.

Waste pollution

In 1985, Spain's 39 million population generated 10.6 million tons, or 265 kg per person per year, of urban solid waste. A high proportion of urban waste disposal is accounted for by uncontrolled dumping, an estimated 46.5 per cent of the total in 1985. Spain's forty composting plants make 700,000 tons of compost each year from 1.5 million tons of waste. Although it is government policy to support schemes for the recovery of raw materials from urban waste, the high cost and energy consumption of reclamation plants are becoming prohibitive. Few towns, and few industries, have equipment for selective material recovery. Despite this, the government has drafted guidelines to encourage local authorities to rationalize urban waste management. More and more recycling – of glass, paper, board, etc. – is taking place yearly. In 1982, for instance, only five towns in Spain had bottle banks, which recovered 837 tons of glass, but, by 1986, 179 towns were recovering 13,318 tons of glass.

Over 10 million tons of industrial waste are generated yearly, and 1.5 million tons of this waste is considered hazardous. Several centres for the treatment of hazardous waste have been established, notably the acid neutralization plant in the Basque region and three oil regeneration plants run by the oil company CAMPSA. Even though 1986 legislation makes contraventions punishable by fines and banning, there are insufficient waste-treatment centres to deal with industrial waste.

The need for regulating industrial waste led to major legislation in 1986. This law includes preventive control measures for waste management – collection, storage, transport, treatment and disposal of waste – and lays down procedures for identifying waste and planning the activities which produce it.

Spain's EC accession made it necessary to bring legislation into line with EC directives. Three aspects of these directives have been adopted in Spain. First, the application of protective measures was widened to cover waste in general. Second, the various administrative bodies engaged in waste management were obliged to introduce integrated management plans. Last, Spain was required to inform the European Commission of the progress of waste-management measures. In line with this provision, central government is responsible for making a national waste management plan, while regional governments have to draw up management plans for their own territories in accordance with the national plan.

Water and sea pollution

In 1985, a new Water Law established a single body to manage surface and ground waters. Serious river pollution increased in the 1980s, and the government responded by allocating grants to the regions to install water-purification plants. Firms have also been awarded subsidies to introduce recycling plants. The proportion of the population served by water-treatment plants went up from 18 per cent in 1980 to 40 per cent in 1986.

The new Water Law, replacing previous legislation dating back to 1879, marks an historic moment for Spain by signalling the introduction of more modern standards into integrated water management, both qualitatively and quantitatively. The fundamental change of direction coincided with Spain's joining the EC and the accompanying obligation to confirm to its directives. Since 1986, extensive action has been taken to reduce the pollution of surface water, notably in the Madrid and Catalonia regions, with other regions working along similar lines. Deficiencies in the treatment of urban waste water have been corrected more rapidly than previously: in 1980, less than 18 per cent of the population was served by a treatment plant while, by 1988, this percentage was climbing above 60 per cent. Nevertheless, most of Spain's major rivers, especially the Ebro, the Guadalquivir and the Guadarrama, are heavily polluted, and serious action is needed to bring these rivers up to standards acceptable to the EC. High levels of pollution are found also in the Mediterranean basins, but this is due more to low rainfall than industrial discharges.

Mass tourism and its attendant industries have helped to create a major threat to Spain's 6,121 km of coastline, 63 per cent of which is rocky terrain, 23 per cent sand, 8 per cent man-made and 4 per cent mudflats. Some 20 per cent of Spain's 3,090 beaches are estimated to be in danger of disappearing from a combination of all factors, including increasing urbanization along coastal areas, which now accommodate 12 million of Spain's population and 65 per cent of industry.

The protection of coastal areas is the subject of legislation approved in 1989. The 1989 law establishes obligations for the protection of the sea – a 100-metre zone, subject to extension – and defines a 'zone of influence' of at least 500 metres, starting from the waterline, which could modify the nature of land and urban planning. The disposal of solid waste and raw sewage is prohibited in the protected area.

Concern over the pollution of seawater and the consequent risks to bathers, an important factor of course in the tourism industry, has resulted in almost obsessive publicity in recent years. Of the 3,090 beaches along the coast, 955 (the most frequented) were analysed. It was found that 91.5 per cent were suitable for bathing, 5.05 per cent were suitable only after taking precautions, and, in 3.45 per cent of cases, bathing was unsafe. This concern led many local authorities to submit requests to the EC to grant the blue flag, symbol of uncontaminated water. More than 100 beaches now fly this flag, with more requests to the EC year by year.

A whole series of programmes has been carried out in recent years to purify the waste water discharged along the Spanish coastline. This has called for sizeable investments. By 1985, 53 billion pesetas had been spent on the Mediterranean coast, with a further 8.5 billion on the Galician coast and 12.5 billion in the Canaries. Since 1985, further massive investment has taken place to monitor sea pollution and clean up the coastline. Thus, of the 190 towns on the Mediterranean coast, approximately two-thirds had sewage treatment plants by the end of 1989, with more under construction.

Forestry and soil erosion

Spain has more natural forest land than any other EC country: the ratio is twice as great as France's, four times as great as Germany's and Italy's, and eight times as great as Portugal's. Concern now focuses on the gradual depletion of natural forests as farmers clear and cultivate woodland sites,

Table 10.2 *Forest fires in Spain*

Year	Number of fires	Total area affected (hectares)
1982	6,443	151,644
1983	4,880	117,599
1984	7,649	164,698
1985	12,284	486,327
1986	7,574	277,513
1987	8,679	145,793
1988	9,595	129,989
1989	20,834	410,181
1990	15,141	200,657
1991	13,025	248,703

Source: ICONA (Institute for Nature Conservation)

and on the poor condition of trees that remain. With 73.8 per cent of the territory in private hands, the government's 1984 legislation to replant land has affected only a small proportion of the total area, and even this has met with criticism from ecology groups unhappy with the methods or species used. Since 1984, most responsibilities for managing wooded land were transferred to the regions, and there are no nationwide affor-estation schemes.

The greatest threat to Spain's natural environment comes from forest fires and their contribution to soil erosion. The 1980s saw a sharp in-crease in the incidence of forest fires, often deliberately started, which, in 1985, damaged an area four times greater than the reafforestation of 1984. Soil erosion now is a bigger problem in Spain than any other EC country. In 1986 alone, 64.2 per cent of Spanish land surface was affected by high or moderate levels of soil erosion. The situation has undoubtedly worsened since then, as is evident from Table 10.2, which clearly shows that, although the damage to land has fluctuated, the number of fires and the area affected have in the early 1990s settled at double or treble the figure of the early 1980s.

At the present rate at which forests in Spain succumb to fires, sooner rather than later there will be the loss of the forests' natural capacity for self-regeneration. Spain's problem is far greater than that of her EC Mediterranean partners: in 1987, while 145,793 hectares were damaged by fire in Spain, the corresponding figure for Italy was 72,152 hectares, for Greece 31,199, and for France 10,087 hectares. Apart from the ecologi-cal damage caused by forest fires, there are immense direct losses of timber, resin and cork. Spain has a strong traditional market for timber and, along with Portugal, accounts for 80 per cent of the global production of cork.

Parks and nature reserves

Although Spain was the first EC country to introduce the concept of national parks in 1916, little was done until 1975 to protect the huge areas of countryside that 10 million people now visit each year. In recent years, the creation of 250 special nature recreation areas for picnicking, camping, bathing, etc., has been accompanied by a national campaign to elevate the status of nature studies.

Flora and fauna

In 1980, legislation created protected areas and game reserves for 300 threatened species, yet forty-three species are currently in danger of extinction from uncontrolled hunting, urbanization, new agricultural methods, etc. These include the Spanish imperial eagle, the black vulture, osprey, brown bear and ibex. Similarly, national legislation (1984) and supplementary regional regulations have done little, until recently, to protect an estimated 1,277 endangered species of endemic plants.

Spain has the widest and most varied selection of flora and fauna in Europe. The climatic characteristics of the Peninsula and the islands permit the existence of productive ecosystems, with rich flora and fauna. Spain is an important crossroads between the continents of Europe and Africa, and therefore a stopping-place for many migratory species, especially birds. A new law, passed in 1989, for the conservation of nature areas and wild plant and animal species contains challenging new regulations for the protection of nature areas and flora and fauna. It remains to be seen, however, whether new legislation can prevent further tourist development of Spain's biggest national park, the Coto Doñana, Europe's biggest sanctuary for birds. This wetland region, in south-west Spain, has seen conservationists locked in a battle with financiers who want to expand tourism in the park. Even though Felipe González spends his summer holidays in the region, there is little evidence of the environmentalists winning this or other similar battles across the country.

A 1988 directive from the EC to Spain to spend 300,000 million pesetas in industry and technology to improve the environment is only one indication of the tremendous strides Spain needs to make in order to catch up with EC partners. Failure to give priority to the environment on the part of government, and a virtually non-existent environment industry, do not suggest that this task is likely to be undertaken in the near future.

It is to be hoped that increasing public concern and EC pressure will cause government and business to devote more attention and resources to Spain's environmental problems.

Conclusion

Spain's biggest environmental problem is raising public consciousness to the level where the average Spaniard perceives environmental damage as an unacceptable facet of progress and modernization. The problem is symbolized by a Minister for Transport and Public Works who also carries the flag for environmental issues! There is, however, substantial evidence to suggest that government and political will on the environment is some way in advance of public thinking. As the Ministry of Tourism tempts constructors and hoteliers to upgrade and relocate supply away from the coast and in places of historical and cultural interest, it does so by placing particular emphasis upon environmental concerns and by launching a 50 million pesetas 'Green Spain' campaign.

The new National Energy Plan of 1991 placed special stress on diversification of the type of fuel used and the strengthening of conservation and environmental protection policies. Three solar energy plants are already in operation in Almeriá, with more under construction. There are seven experimental wind-energy centres across the country, while research into renewable energies is expanding, e.g. the OLAS-1,000 project to produce electricity from marine energy. By 1990, renewable energies in Spain accounted for 3.5 per cent of total energy consumption and the proportion was rising rapidly.

The Spanish Minister in charge of the environment, José Borell, recognized in 1991 that Spain would need to spent 1.2 billion pesetas in a 5-year period to comply with EC environmental legislation. His confidence that this would take place is perhaps an indicator of changing government priorities with regard to the environment rather than a predictor of what would actually be achieved.

11 Business, business people and enterprise

Introduction

The legacy of underinvestment, overmanning, and poor training has been outlined in previous chapters, as have the tremendous efforts made by the business community and by government to overcome these deficiencies. Infrastructural weakness – roads, railways, etc. – is, as we have seen, also being addressed. Spanish industry will have to wait well beyond 1992 to reap the full rewards of such labours, despite individual company successes. It remains to be seen, though, how the essential framework of a business culture founded upon a proliferation of small and medium-sized firms will withstand the growing intensity of competition from Europe's (and the world's) multinationals.

Spain appears to be putting its faith in the business people sent forth to compete in the open markets of post-1992. The priority given to education by successive González governments represents an attempt to turn out from the education system a more rounded and internationally-minded product capable of flourishing in the changing capitalist market-place. The success or failure of this new generation of entrepreneurs and decision-makers may well be a major determinant of Spain's economic and political standing at the start of the twenty-first century.

Social trends and characteristics

From 1992 on earnings, employment and consumption were expected to continue to rise in Spain, although more moderately perhaps than in the preceding years of spectacular growth. Spaniards had seen their standard of living improve quite considerably in the 1980s, although a continuing high level of unemployment was an uncomfortable statistic. In a 1991 comparative survey of employment provision in the EC member states, *The European* ranked Spain in eighth place in terms of employee conditions (with Germany first, France third and the UK in ninth position). Employees in Spain do, however, have a government-guaranteed and inflation-linked 'minimum interprofessional salary', as well as 30 days' minimum paid holiday per year and 15 days off for marriage!

Rising standards in health care and education since the democratic transition have been the result of government measures to establish a social welfare state on a par with those of her EC partners. Spain has the second highest ratio (after Italy) of doctors per head of population and life expectancy rose from the 1950 level of fifty-nine for men and sixty-four for women to the 1984 level of seventy-four for men and eighty for women. Ownership of cars, telephones, computers, etc., is rapidly growing but is still some way short of that in the northern EC countries. Interest rates are among the highest in the EC, although reductions are planned, and indirect taxation is set to increase as the Spanish VAT rate of 12 per cent is forced up to conform with EC directives. New lower rates of personal income tax are being introduced in stages, however, with the top rate of 56 per cent planned to go down to 50 per cent and the minimum rate of 25 per cent set to reduce to 18 per cent.

Spaniards are among the most consumerist of peoples. They enjoy spending money and have one of the lowest savings ratings of any country in Europe. The average Spaniard expects to eat out at a restaurant with family or friends several times a week, and does not regard this as an extravagance. The Spanish business executive, along with many blue-collar workers, will expect to own, or aspire to own, a holiday or second home, which may be modest, close to the sea or in the mountains, and which will be used regularly at weekends and during the summer holidays, when at least a month's break is taken. It would not be a truism to say that the Spanish 'work hard and play hard'. They socialize until the early hours of the morning quite regularly, and often in the company of their family, including children. Although comparisons are difficult, they probably sleep less than most of their European neighbours and, apart from holiday periods, the siesta is no longer observed. Above all, Spaniards are usually generous hosts, both with their time and with their pockets.

Spain's retail revolution

One of the biggest sea-changes in Spain's recent history has been the retail revolution, which is gradually educating the Spanish customer away from the expectation of a traditionally individual and personal service to acceptance of self-service. The concept of self-service in Spain is only 30 years old. The first **almacén** (large department store) opened in 1956, the first **supercercado** (supermarket) in 1960 and the first **hipermercado** (hypermarket) in Barcelona in 1973. In addition, approximately three-quarters of all supermarkets and **autoservicios** (self-service stores) have only opened in the last 15 years. Since the 1980s, the retail revolution has

Table 11.1 *Main hypermarkets in Spain*

Name	Ownership
Pryca	Carrefour and Grupo March (French)
Continente	Promodes and BBV (French)
Alcampo	Auchamps (French)
Hipercor	El Corte Inglés (Spanish)

Source: Consumer Spain '91

spread very quickly as a result of a rise in consumer expenditure and foreign investment. Small traditional shops are still important but, with a lengthy chain of agents and an expensive distribution system, they are now in decline. At the turn of the decade, it was estimated that 95 per cent of points of sale accounted for 54 per cent of sales volume, while 5 per cent (the self-service sector) accounted for 46 per cent. **Galerías de alimentación** (covered markets) are also still used in Spain.

The rise of hypermarkets, often referred to as **los hiper**, is particularly noticeable. In 1992, they numbered about 150, with more planned, and they have changed the nature of routine shopping by shifting emphasis toward edge-of-town and out-of-town centres. Most stores belong to one of four companies, which account for 75 per cent of all hypermarket sales. They are listed in order of size in Table 11.1.

New shopping centres have also arrived on the Spanish scene, with twelve built or planned since 1988, including three in Madrid. The largest of these, Parquesur in the capital city, covers 140,000 m² and has 320 shops, among them Alcampo, C & A and the department store Galerías Preciados (controlled by the British Mountleigh group), as well as 6,000 parking spaces.

According to a 1990 Nielsen Survey, the share of food sales from traditional small shops was only 25 per cent, compared with 75 per cent in 1975. Many small shops have now adopted survival strategies such as specialization and niche marketing, e.g. boutiques and delicatessens, and formation of associations for bulk purchasing. The leading Spanish retailers in terms of turnover are listed in Table 11.2.

Business attitudes and characteristics

Understanding how Spanish people conduct business is as important an element in a successful business relationship with Spain as good communicative skills in the foreign language. Spaniards are on the whole as

Table 11.2 *Leading Spanish retailers*

Name	Type	Sales turnover in 1988 (billion pesetas)
El Corte Inglés	Department store	435
Pryca	Hypermarket	213
Continente	Hypermarket	147
Alcampo	Hypermarket	122
Galerías Preciados	Department store	81
Mercadona	Self-service store	81
Simago	Self-service store	55

Source: Consumer Spain '91

much concerned to preserve their own distinctive traditions and characteristics as a people as they are to modernize their country. The Spanish tradition of spending time with people in social situations, such as evening drinks and tapas, or an evening meal, is of crucial importance in developing business relationships. Business people in Spain do not appreciate the more formal, desk-bound approach to discussion and decision-making characteristic of the Anglo-Saxon executive. In Spain, the development of a good business relationship is very much tied up with the development of a good personal relationship. Mutual trust and understanding are regarded as very important, and social situations facilitate their development.

Misunderstanding or even conflict between Spanish and British business people tends to revolve around a different interpretation of time. Despite their *mañana* image, Spaniards are very time-conscious; they do not, however, regard it as a waste of time to take a lengthy mid-morning break at the cafeteria with colleagues, eat a full 2-hour lunch, or to spend an evening sampling tapas before eating an evening meal, which may not start until after 10 pm. On the contrary, such social occasions both cement the personal relationship and often provide the informal forum where formal decisions are forged. This people-friendly, apparently time-consuming approach can frustrate non-Spaniards, who often like to move more directly to a decision-making situation; Spaniards, on the other hand, may prefer a series of preliminary meetings over a period of months to establish the integrity of potential partners. In addition, considerable stamina and enthusiasm are recommended for the 'night on the town', which may follow the evening meal that finished at midnight! A working lunch with sandwiches is therefore not appropriate in Spain, where there is also no custom of dinner parties or home entertainment

Table 11.3   *Statutory bank holidays in Spain*

---

1 January (*Día del Año Nuevo*).
6 January (*Epifanía/Día de los Reyes Magos*).
19 March (*Día de San José*).
Good Friday (*Viernes Santo*).
1 May (Labour Day – *Fiesta del Trabajo*).
15 August (Assumption – *Asunción de la Virgén*).
12 October (National Day – *Día de la Hispanidad/Día de la Raza*).
1 November (All Saints' Day – *Todos los Santos*).
6 December (Constitution Day – *Día de la Constitución*).
8 December (Immaculate Conception – *Día de la Inmaculada Concepción*).
25 December (*Día de Navidad*).

---

of business colleagues or clients. Working breakfasts similarly are not yet common.

In Spain, friends, families and colleagues go out together to eat and drink in hotels, bars and restaurants. That you are not invited home is no slight, merely the norm. Naturally, there are do's and don'ts in terms of topics of conversation. The Spanish will appreciate the demonstration of real interest in and knowledge of any aspect of Spanish life, politics included, by the visitor. However, despite the fact that most Spaniards are very liberal-minded, the subjects of Franco and religion, irrespective of the irreligious nature of the hosts, are best avoided.

Another area of frequent misunderstanding between non-Spaniards and Spanish business people is the subject of holidays and working hours. Spain, like most other EC countries, has more statutory holidays than the UK. The statutory holidays generally observed are listed in Table 11.3. Other holidays vary according to the province, but the legal number of holidays allowed in a year is fourteen. When a bank holiday falls on a Thursday or Tuesday, Spaniards usually take the intervening Friday or Monday off (known as **hacer puente**). The proximity of the holidays on 6 December and 8 December means that a holiday of a week or more may be taken at this time, making it difficult for businesses to be contacted.

Most business people take their summer holidays in August (for the whole month) or in July, with occasionally an overlap between the two. July–August is therefore a period when little business is done. In addition, from June to September, many business people spend weekends in a second or holiday home, and this affects business on Friday afternoons.

School and university holidays vary somewhat according to region, but the long summer vacation usually lasts from the end of June to mid-September (schools) and from the end of June to mid-October (higher education).

The working hours of foreign companies in Spain are usually from 8.30 am or 9 am to 5.30 pm or 6 pm, with an hour for lunch. Many Spanish companies have a longer lunch period, often 2 hours, and a later closing, between 7 pm and 8 pm. Between June and September most companies follow an **horario intensivo** (intensive timetable) of seven continuous hours' work from 8 am to 3 pm.

Female managers

In 1993, women constituted 35 per cent of the working population in Spain, 58 per cent of university students and 40 per cent of professional and technical workers. However, women occupied only 14 per cent of managerial positions in state-owned industries and only 5 per cent in private enterprise. According to a report of the International Labour Organization (ILO), at the current rate of progress it will take women in Spain 475 years to achieve parity with men in the upper reaches of executive decision-making.

From 1983 to 1993, the number of working women increased by 6.7 per cent, while male employment fell by 6.2 per cent; thus 1,539,100 women joined the workforce, compared with a total of 306,800 men. Despite this, the number of unemployed women rose to 1,494,100 in 1993, approximately 49 per cent of the total unemployed. The figures demonstrate the problems women face in securing jobs and the low level of female senior executives.

Female managers who have reached the upper echelons of management in Spain claim that women are allowed to progress to middle management positions but not higher. Statistics support such assertions. Thus, of the top 160 companies, only two are chaired by women, and one of these, Ana Botín, chairperson of the Banco de Santander, is the daughter of the bank's owner. Only twenty-one women hold directorships of banks, whereas there are more than 1,000 bank directors across the country. Only five of the country's 133 newspapers are run by women, although the figure is higher, unsurprisingly, in the field of women's and interior design magazines, with fifty-nine of 439 publications managed by women.

An identikit picture of the Spanish female manager is as follows: between 25 and 45 years of age, university-educated, fluent in English and / or French, completed management training, especially in marketing, information technology or personnel. The majority of female managers (six out of ten) have worked their way up into positions of responsibility in the same company, although on average they earn 20 per cent less than male equivalents. Most are either single, or marry and have children when they are older. In May 1993, *The European* newspaper carried a profile of a successful female executive, Nieves Sarria, managing director of Ibermática, a medium-sized software company. Educated in business science at the University of Deusto, Nieves Sarria had been managing director of Ibermática, which employs 600 people, for 3 years. Sarria was quoted as saying that the position of Spanish women in top jobs has changed slowly but progressively: 'I don't believe that there are differences between women and men when it comes to running a business. But the economic crisis is triggering conservative reactions among executives when deciding to hire or promote women to executive posts'.

The response of Spanish business to 1992

The Spanish business community's attitude to the EC's Single Market has been characterized by guarded apprehension alongside keen anticipation. The apprehension is based upon the painful adjustments already made since the demise of Franco and entry into the EC in 1986. Accompanying the apprehension, however, is a realistic acceptance of the price Spanish industry must pay if it is to be a serious major international competitor. Investment in modern plant and machinery has been rapid, as the business community reflects the near-unanimous enthusiasm for Spain's full participation in the EC among the general population. Such enthusiasm has meant that, within the institutions of the EC, Spaniards have quickly acquired a reputation as whole-hearted Europeans.

Spanish manufacturing labour costs in the late 1980s were only half the level of former West Germany's, and Spain's wage levels were the lowest in the EC, after Greece and Portugal. Spanish business therefore had a head start over its competitors. Even though labour costs rose in line with inflation in 1990, 1991 and 1992, as long as real wage rises do not exceed productivity growth, Spanish business can hope to continue expanding in the mid-1990s. New planned legislation on restrictive business practices will further enhance competition, already galvanized by the lifting of import quotas and the halving of tariffs since EC accession. Spain's historical links with Latin America and her friendly relations with the Arab world are other factors that give Spanish business a distinct trading advantage over EC partners, a fact acknowledged by some foreign companies, which bought into Spain precisely to gain a foothold in markets notoriously difficult to penetrate.

No one should underestimate the positive motivational influences on the business community that the worldwide fashionableness of Spain in the past few years has generated. Spanish fashion (*diseño*) and the complex socio-cultural phenomenon of the *movida* – an explosion of the plastic and fine arts combined with a youth pop-cult – have been exported successfully to other EC countries. A proliferation of fashion shows and exhibitions in the major cities of Europe (e.g. Harrod's 1-month 'made in Spain' exhibition in 1988) has been accompanied by renewed enthusiasm for Spanish artists. In 1988, for instance, plays by Lorca were staged to great acclaim in Paris and London, Italy fêted some of Spain's best known writers, and the film director Pedro Almodóvar became a cult figure. *Newsweek's* issue of 23 May 1988, a special devoted to Spain, captured the mood succinctly with its front cover picture of Felipe González and a caption that read: 'Spain: Racing into the Future. Europe's Tortoise turns into a Hare'.

Some commentators believe that the conglomeration of events in 1992 – the Olympics, Expo '92, Madrid's stint as cultural centre of Europe, etc. – has already helped to forge a unity of national purpose in Spain as the country battled successfully to meet a deadline of the kind that Spaniards, well known for their improvisation rather than their planning, excel at fulfilling. Sponsorship on a massive scale was secured from Spanish and foreign companies for the events of 1992. The organizational successes of the Olympics and Expo attracted massive publicity worldwide, representing a major public relations coup for Spain. Coca-Cola was the biggest sponsor of the Barcelona Olympics, and also sponsored the Spanish team. Expo '92's main sponsors were the Spanish banks – Banco de Bilbao y Vizcaya, Español Central de Créditos, Banco Central Hispanomericano and the Banco Exterior de España. Even before 1992, Spain was the second most successful country in the world, behind the US, in terms of sponsorship income. Clearly, the entrepreneurial spirit is thriving and looking forward eagerly to all the various opportunities afforded post-1992.

The Spanish entrepreneur

The Spanish media have appeared to be obsessed with the implications of 1992, not least of course because the completion of the Single Market coincided happily with the Barcelona Olympics, Expo '92 in Seville, and the fifth centenary of Columbus's discovery of America. While there is little evidence to suggest that Spanish industry as a whole has examined its own response to 1992 with the same thoroughness, nonetheless a new breed of younger, business-school-trained, European-minded executives is emerging in enough Spanish companies to encourage longer-term optimism. Symbols are potent in Spain and the new captains of industry look to the successful example of Spain's 'Lois' jeans in the 1980s, where, against the odds, a Spanish product took on French and Italian fashions in one case and the jeans market in the other. In both cases, hard-and-fast rules of reinvesting were observed by a single shareholder company that put a high premium on advertising and kept growing.

A new breed of business executives genuinely aspires to establish Spanish business in European markets, while defending domestic interests against foreign incursions. A recent study, published by the business consultants SRU, gives hope that the aspiration can become a reality. According to the study, the ideal executive to lead companies into the post-1992 Europe will be from a small country, be multilingual, have a flexible mind and social brilliance, will come from a multicultural family, will be a male graduate of a business school, and will almost certainly not be British.

This identikit picture could describe the new executive breed in Spain, usually from the wealthy classes, often with an MBA from a US university. José Barroso, 34-year-old head of the multimillion-peseta enterprise Don Algodón, with over 100 fashion shops in Spain, fits the picture exactly. Barroso, from a comfortable upper-middle-class Madrid family, borrowed £350 from a bank when he was 17 years old, started selling T-shirts to school friends, and, at 20, travelled to Italy to bid successfully for the Benetton franchise in Spain. In the 1990s, with plans to extend the Don Algodón operation across Europe, Barroso's company – with the successful example of Lois jeans to follow – seems certain to be one of the first of a whole succession of Spanish companies to take full advantage of the opportunities afforded by the Single Market.

Small companies and start-ups

With increased competition from within and without the EC, small companies in Spain have had to develop their entrepreneurial skills very rapidly in recent years. Many companies have gone to the wall, but many more have displayed considerable enterprise in order to be competitive. The insularity of the Franco era has been cast aside as small firms combine with other small firms in Spain or aboard in order to achieve economies of scale and maximize shared enterprise. This does not necessarily imply a full joint venture or networking arrangement, but may be a strategic alliance in a particular market or sector, i.e. a specific agreement to co-operate within defined parameters.

Small Spanish companies have traditionally been very reluctant to link up, but in recent years many of them have been forging strategic alliances in order to survive. The message coming from increased EC competition is 'ally or die', and companies have combined to co-operate over specific programmes, e.g. export, purchase of materials, product development, shared research, etc. In this respect, it could be said that the PYMES are emulating the large companies in Spain, which have increasingly gone in for transnational operations, e.g. the Repsol–Agip link; the

Nunni automobile alliance, which links General Motors with Toyota; and the EC Airbus project.

There are numerous examples of successful alliances of small, often family companies. For instance, Carlos Velasco e Hijos, Conservas Antonio Echevarría and Conservas Dufer are three Cantabrian companies engaged in the packaging of fish. They have formed a consortium for the purposes of fish purchase and export but continue as competitors in the domestic market. In Spain, the **Instituto de Comercio Exterior** (Institute of Foreign Trade or ICEX) and the chambers of commerce have taken a leading role in forming export consortia of PYMES. More importantly for any small company starting up in Spain, the **Instituto de Pequeñas y Medianas Empresas** (Institute of Small and Medium-Sized Firms or IMPI) provides concrete aid to consortia of small companies. Within the **Plan de Promoción de Diseño, Calidad y Moda** (plan for the promotion of design, quality and fashion), IMPI promotes agreements in the sectors of confection, jewellery, footwear, furniture, ceramics, toys, etc. Toy manufacturers in particular display the trend toward strategic alliances.

Strategic alliances are not without financial implications, of course. Additional management costs may be incurred, but again organizations such as IMPI can help. IMPI participates, for example, in collectives formed by PYMES, usually for a 3-year period and often in research, quality control and design. Alliances crossing national boundaries may also be eligible for support from a variety of EC programmes. The most relevant perhaps to small companies is the EC BRITE programme, which awards subsidies for research and development and includes a sub-programme, CRAFT, which is specifically designed to assist consortia of small companies.

For a small foreign company, starting up in Spain need not be difficult as long as a number of sensible steps are followed. Chapters 12 and 13 provide a thorough guide to penetrating the Spanish business culture, but it is worth making at this juncture a brief checklist of the steps that should be taken:

- Allocate a member (or members) of staff with the time and interest to research the Spanish market.
- Approach organizations with the expertise and the willingness to help, e.g. the Department of Trade and Industry, the local chamber of commerce.
- Consider joining a trade mission to Spain to take advantage of group reductions on travel and accommodation.
- Be prepared to commit finances to researching the Spanish market.
- Consider producing promotional material, e.g. leaflets, in Spanish so as to facilitate contacts in Spain.

- Remember that the regions offer start-up incentives and financial concessions that may vary.
- Use organizations such as the DTI and chambers of commerce to find a suitable local agent if required and/or a Spanish lawyer who understands the UK.
- Plan well ahead to learn or improve Spanish language skills if intending to establish a permanent presence in Spain.

Small companies and new technologies

Although many small firms in Spain, which are often family firms, do not have the money for technological updating, the interest in employing the latest technologies is usually great, and is backed up by a number of national and regional initiatives targeted at small firms. An example of the kind of help that may be provided at regional level is to be found in the low-interest loans, R & D concessions and cash grants made available to small and medium-sized companies by the **Instituto Madrileño para el Desarrollo Económico** or **IMADE** (Madrid Economic and Development Agency). IMADE, which services the Madrid regional government, also provides subsidies for training programmes to new ventures, whether Spanish or foreign.

It is also possible for small companies to take on new employees who can bring to the firm expertise in the new technologies. The central government **Instituto Nacional para el Empleo** or **INEM** (National Institute for Employment) has been devoting considerable resources in recent years to training for the unemployed. Centres have been established throughout Spain, and emphasis has been put on training in the new technologies. Since half of INEM's budget derives from the European Social Fund, it works in close conjunction with regional governments and the European Commission.

Conclusion

Spanish society has undergone a profound transformation since the 1970s as the rapprochement with Western Europe has seen Spaniards adopting the attitudes and the tastes of their EC neighbours. Spanish business people have, in many ways, been in the vanguard of 'Europeanization', since industry and commerce have driven the Spanish economy and society forward. Nonetheless, a distinctive 'Spanish' way of doing things has been proudly preserved, and a proper understanding of Spain's business culture is predicated upon acknowledging this distinctiveness.

If the 1980s saw Spain undertake painful but necessary modernization and streamlining of industry, 1992 was a powerful trigger to increase entrepreneurial endeavours and compete successfully in the wider European and international marketplace. There are numerous opportunities for small companies to take advantage of regional, national and European schemes to update their technology, to tie up with other small companies, and to internationalize their operations. Start-ups in Spain have never been so well supported, and the business and political environment welcomes the interest of non-Spanish companies and investors. The other side of the coin is that Spanish entrepreneurs have already begun to make their mark elsewhere in Europe. With a steady rise in the number of business executives on the employment market, often with management training, this trend is likely to accelerate in the next decade.

12 Penetrating the Spanish business culture I – the overall picture

Introduction

Opportunities of penetrating the Spanish business culture need to be set within the context of the impact of EC integration. Earlier chapters dealt with this in greater detail. It is, however, crucial to remember that there is near-unanimous enthusiasm for the benefits of EC membership among ordinary Spaniards. Indeed, the Socialist government won its second general election in 1986 largely upon its success in achieving EC membership for Spain some months earlier.

The terms of Spain's EC entry meant a variety of transitional arrangements for full economic integration. In agriculture, the transitional period was 7 years, except for fruit and vegetables (10 years), with special conditions for wine and olive oil. The banks and financial services also faced a 7-year transition, in which European banks were limited to a maximum of three branches in the first 4 years, rising gradually to eight branches in the 7th year, with no restrictions in place after this period. The terms for industrial and commercial union provided for a gradual dismantling of tariff barriers over 7 years. Thus, the first tariff cut was 10 per cent in March 1986, followed by 12.5 per cent in January 1987, 15 per cent in 1988 and 1989, 12.5 per cent in 1990, 1991 and 1992, and a final 10 per cent in 1993.

In an important sense, 1993, the first year of completion of the Single Market, merely meant 'more of the same' to Spanish industry. In other words, more imports from abroad at increasingly competitive prices and more interest from foreign firms in buying into or buying out Spanish firms.

The market for electrical household goods best exemplifies the problem. Already in the years since EC entry, Spain has experienced an invasion of imported goods – Italian washing machines, German television sets, French refrigerators and Dutch hi-fi equipment. The gradual reduction of tariff barriers and import taxes since 1986 has meant that any product carrying a 100-peseta tariff before 1986 paid only 35 pesetas in 1989 but nothing in 1993.

The retail chain store giant El Corte Inglés in 1989 signed an agreement with an Italian producer of electrical goods to supply its stores. Previously El Corte Inglés had always used Spanish manufacturers. The majority of Spain's supermarkets have foreign capital behind them, with French interests predominant, and, with the gradual removal of tariff barriers, are retailing more imported goods.

Spain's traditionally strong electricity-generation sector illustrates the threat to Spanish ownership of companies. A thousand companies make up the sector, with 70 per cent privately owned and 30 per cent in state hands. Twenty-one firms, however, produce 98 per cent of the total, in which 1.5 million small shareholders have a stake. The market is vulnerable to rationalization and foreign intervention, with the German company RWE leading the way.

Foreign investment opportunities

Inward foreign investment was almost non-existent in the Spain of the 1950s, was still small in the 1960s, began to grow in the 1970s and the first half of the 1980s, but only rose sharply after 1986. Net foreign investment grew from 199 billion pesetas in 1982 to 1,830 billion pesetas in 1990, a nine-fold increase explained by Spain's low labour costs, national and regional fiscal and financial incentives, a growing domestic market, political stability, EC membership, Latin American and Arab links, and a strong peseta. Liberalization of foreign investment in the 1970s, and especially since 1986, which allows the transfer abroad of unlimited capital, profits and dividends, has placed Spain in fourth position worldwide in respect of volume of investment, after the US, the UK and France. The only formal restrictions on investment relate to the defence industry, telecommunications, radio and television, and the gambling industry.

Since Spain entered the EC, there has been a move by investors from industrial sectors toward financial institutions, insurance companies, real estate activities and services rendered to companies. The trend is clearly seen in Table 12.1.

EC countries are the main investors, especially Germany, The Netherlands, France and the UK, followed by the US and Japan. In 1989, the UK became the largest single source of direct foreign investment, a position maintained since then. A major part of Spain's inward investment has been in the Madrid and Catalonia regions (with Japanese investment by Nissan, Suzuki and Sanyo particularly strong in the latter), which together have accounted for between 40 per cent and 60 per cent of total

Table 12.1   *Direct foreign investment by sector (% of total)*

	1984	1990
Financial institutions, insurance etc.	17.5	46.5
Mineral and by-product extraction	14.8	12.7
Miscellaneous manufacturing	11.6	12.1
Business, hotels and restaurants	16.9	9.5
Energy and water	0.6	3.5
Construction	1.3	2.2
Transport and communications	0.5	1.5

Source: *Anuario El País*

foreign investment since 1986. As a footnote, outward foreign investment has also grown very rapidly from a very low base and again has been directed mostly to the EC and the US, especially in financial services, commerce and the hotel and restaurant trade.

Although global foreign investment is growing yearly, Spain still wants more, to compensate for limited sources of indigenous capital and the historic tendency of Spanish banks (though this is changing) to prefer to invest in real estate rather than in industry. In 1990, foreigners in effect owned 10 per cent of Spain, accounting for 9.3 per cent of GDP, as more foreign firms bought into or bought out Spanish firms. Many small and medium-sized Spanish companies, especially family firms, are ripe for purchase: they are relatively cheap and do not have the finance necessary for technological updating. Opportunities abound in every sector, as can be seen from a sample selection of foreign investment initiatives in recent years. State-owned car manufacturers SEAT and ENASA have passed into German hands. Banks have changed ownership, with, for example, a 75 per cent stake in Banco Atlántico taken by the Arab Aresbank. In construction, the Arabs and Italians have been to the fore, with Gianni Agnelli now owning one-third of HUARTE. In food and drink, the brewers El Aguila now have Heineken as major shareholder, while Benedetti from Italy owns 27 per cent of the food manufacturer Pascual Hermanos.

Household names in Spain therefore have 'gone foreign', and the trend is accelerating. Spain's traditionally strong electricity sector, comprising 1,000 companies, is vulnerable to rationalization and foreign intervention. British companies such as Wiggins Teape have shown how to invest successfully in Spain. The British firm was eager to purchase CEASA, a wood-pulp manufacturer owned by the Banco Español de Crédito. The route chosen was to form a new Spanish company in order to make a

100 per cent investment through the acquisition of shares. Wiggins Teape reports that three essential steps were crucial to its success. First, it employed a first-class Spanish lawyer who understood Britain, not a British lawyer who claimed to understand Spain or Spanish. Then it found a first-class accountant and third, obtained the backing of a bank.

The Spanish government has also actively welcomed foreign investment in state-owned firms (see pp. 24–26). Having spent the 1980s rationalizing and streamlining many industries in the public holding company, the INI (National Institute for Industry), the government announced a further 150-billion-pesetas restructuring plan in late 1991. The plan aimed to capitalize and privatize the healthier companies in INI, while maintaining the chronically indebted ones under the government wing. It classified public-sector companies by profitability and described acceptable candidates for complete or partial privatization as the 'nucleus of opportunities'. Companies forming this nucleus – the list included, among others, the electricity giant ENDESA, the aluminium manufacturers INESPAL, and the Spanish airline IBERIA – would receive 150 billion pesetas. Additional funding would be achieved by floating the stock of selected companies and by increasing the capital of those already quoted on the stockmarket. The expectation was that the sale of these companies, or the inclusion of private capital in them, would help boost their competitiveness and productivity.

The service sector in particular offers considerable investment prospects. This sector in Spain is the most dynamic sector of the economy and the most significant component of GDP (54.6 per cent in 1991). Foreign investments have been directed mainly at the financial institutions, insurance, transport and the hotel and catering trade. Many Spanish firms in this sector are small and require innovation, organization and management. Opportunities are therefore abundant, particularly in insurance and advertising. The insurance market, while expanding rapidly, has obvious room for further growth when 40 per cent of Spaniards have not yet taken out an insurance policy (see pp. 48–49). Similarly, the advertising industry has been growing by an average of 20 per cent per year since 1988, with all forms of media increasing turnover.

An interesting case study is that of Addison Design, a British company, which was chosen by RENFE, the Spanish national railway network, to create the interior design for the high-speed train, the AVE, seen as the flagship of Spain's new railway system. Addison's project team included ergonomists, transportation and interior designers, and design specialists from other consultancies in Britain and Spain. Addison's Spanish experience also encompassed the Spanish dry pet foods manufacturer Purina, which came to Addison for help in creating the identity packaging and merchandising that would launch it successfully in the Spanish and other European markets. In both cases, Addison's ability to work in and manage multicultural, multiskilled teams was regarded as its greatest strength. Above all, the ability to communicate in Spanish and show an understanding of Spanish culture, has been a fundamental factor in the company's success in Spain. Addison's part in the AVE project is an indication both of opportunities for foreign companies in this service sector and of the Spanish interest in design.

There are, of course, a number of important considerations that a potential foreign investor should bear in mind before investing in Spain. The main ones are as follows:

- With very few exceptions, prior administrative verification is no longer needed for direct investments, regardless of the percentage of share-holding in the Spanish company.
- The trade unions in Spain are not against foreign investment, and the labour movement welcomes it to the extent that it relieves unemployment.
- Tax concessions are available to the foreign investor under the same terms as for Spanish companies. There are eight main kinds of concession:

1 Tax credits for investment and as employment incentives.
2 Promotion of new technology.
3 Tax reduction for investment in specific industries and in designated **zonas promocionables** (promotional areas).
4 Tax reductions for investment in enterprises under productivity agreements.
5 Tax benefits on mergers and spin-offs.
6 Local tax concessions.
7 Tax benefits for joint ventures and regional industrial development corporations.
8 Tax benefits granted to certain industries.

- Regional incentives are available through central government, regional governments and local government, especially in regions of the country that have not benefited from industrial expansion or are experiencing economic difficulties. There are two main groups of incentives:

1 Tax incentives, comprising a reduction of local taxes, relating to the establishment or expansion of industrial plants, based on location, and a reduction of the business licence tax during the construction and start-up period.
2 Non-tax incentives (by far the larger), comprising subsidies, varying between 20 per cent and 50 per cent of total investment;

subsidies of interest on loans; and reductions of up to 50 per cent of employer social security contributions.

- Special-use company incentives are also available for investments in mining, gas and oil exploration; investments in research and development programmes; and investments by publishing houses, exporting companies, individual business people and industrial banks and entities engaged in promoting companies.

Researching the Spanish market

Despite numerous individual cases of British companies successfully entering the Spanish market, in general terms there has been little awareness of the available opportunities. A 1989 CBI conference entitled 'Spain – Europe's new economic miracle' reported the reluctance of the British business community to participate in trade fairs to Spain, despite the boom. In the intervening years, the British Embassy, the Department of Trade and Industry and the British Chamber of Commerce have all worked hard to rectify the situation, and, in the words of a DTI video, to put the 'Spotlight on Spain'.

A good way to research the Spanish market is to make use of the British government's export services. The Department of Trade and Industry, together with the Foreign and Commonwealth Office (FCO), provide, through Overseas Trade Services, a wide range of services for UK exporters. The obvious starting point is to identify the best person or people in the company qualified or able to spend time, effort and resources in researching the market. The DTI is able to provide names, addresses, contact points, and lists of agents and distributors in Spain, and it also publishes regular reports on Spain and on a variety of market sectors.

Two specific services have already assisted many UK firms and are worth outlining. The first is the Market Information Enquiry Service, in which research on a requested area of the Spanish market is carried out by FCO commercial staff. The second service is called the Export Representatives' Service. Appointing an overseas representative is a key decision, and this service provides a comprehensive package of information and specific recommendations of potential agents and distributors. A firm using this service will need to provide full information about itself and its requirements or aspirations, so that the information can be passed on to the British Embassy in Madrid, where potential agents and/or distributors will be interviewed on the company's behalf. The two services mentioned above attract a charge, while a number of others are provided free to exporters.

The next crucial stage is to visit Spain for oneself to pursue contacts. It is important to maintain direct contact with the market. You will need to gauge at first hand the potential for the market and assess methods of entry and prospective partners/agents/customers, etc. One of the best ways of doing this is to join a trade mission to Spain, organized by the DTI, chambers of commerce or other bodies. Trade missions are perhaps especially suitable for small- to medium-sized companies because of clear financial and administrative advantages. Savings on group travel and accommodation can be made, while trade missions can also facilitate introductions to the right contacts in local government and the media. Trade missions may assist with the language barrier by furnishing interpreters and arranging translation of trade literature into Spanish. In addition, a follow-up report is usually written.

Examples of the success of trade missions to Spain are the missions organized by the Scottish Council Development and Industry (SCDI) in June 1988, June 1990 and June 1991. Fifty-one companies participated in the last mission, twenty-four of them visiting Spain for the first time. The value of immediate business arising from the missions was put at £472,000, while the value of continuing business generated was estimated at £3,798,000.

As well as the British Chamber of Commerce in Spain, which has excellent up-to-date information, its counterpart, the Spanish Chamber of Commerce in the UK, also produces very useful booklets. The national chambers of commerce work in concert to publish a bi-monthly booklet in Britain listing companies interested in the Spanish market, and information on potential partners and on trade fairs. The British Embassy and British Council Offices in Spain are also helpful, while the Economist Intelligence Unit (EIU) publishes a variety of journals and reports giving information on business trends and on specific sectors. Euromonitor also publishes reports, and produced a hefty volume, *Consumer Spain '91*, which is essential reading for any business contemplating the Spanish market and contains a lengthy section entitled 'Sources of Information in Spain'. The *Financial Times, The Guardian* and *The Economist* have all produced regular surveys on Spain in recent years, and these are a useful source for private (and free!) research.

Finally, the EC can provide practical advice and assistance in a number of areas. Currently, Spain and the UK collaborate in more than twenty projects under the EUREKA programme and a whole host of other EC collaborative schemes such as BRITE, ESPIRIT, etc. The British Embassy has identified areas in which research and development are taking place in Spain and the UK and in which industrial technological collaboration might be useful, particularly in sharing often enormous costs, and which might lead to participation in EUREKA and other industrially led European projects. The main areas identified include microelectronics, new materials, information technology and engineering, advanced manufacturing systems and biotechnology. Clearly, the EC has given priority to high-tech, precisely the area where Spain is most interested and needs help. The EC COMET scheme, which promotes co-operation between enterprises and higher education institutions in the different member states, would allow, for instance, a Spanish MBA student to work in a British company on a 6-month or 1-year placement. The British Council, in conjunction with the Spanish Ministry of Education and Science, also administers an **Acciones Integradas** (integrated actions) scheme, which supports collaborative research at universities and public research bodies.

Direct exporting

Spain has been running a trading deficit since the mid-1980s, as its export drive, while successful, has failed to match the flood of imports. There has, though, been a major shift in trade towards EC countries since the early 1980s. In 1982, only 32 per cent of the value of all imports came from the EC, compared with 57 per cent in 1991. Exports to the EC also increased, from 49 per cent of total revenue in 1982 to over 67 per cent in 1991. Spain's leading trade partners in 1991 were, in this order, France, Germany, Italy, USA and the UK.

The sectors showing the biggest increases in imports in 1991 were food and drink, furs and textiles, and optical, photographic and musical instruments, although it must be remembered that almost every sector showed a considerable rise. In exports, Spain was most successful in raising exports of cars and tractors, fuels and mineral oils, machinery and electrical appliances, and vegetable produce.

Spain is the UK's eighth largest export market, while the UK is Spain's fourth largest. UK exporters have begun to make steady inroads into Spanish markets but start from a very low base. Most British firms established in Spain in the 1930s pulled out in the early years of Franco's rule, unlike French, German and US companies, which kept a large Spanish presence.

The Department of Trade and Industry has drawn up the following list of priority sectors in recent years:

- Machine tools.
- Telecommunications and broadcasting equipment.
- Scientific instruments and laboratory equipment.
- Building materials.
- Computer software and informatics.
- Airport and related equipment.
- Food and drink.

- Pollution control and environmental technology.
- Automotive components, garage and forecourt equipment.

There are numerous stories of successful exporting to Spain by British companies since Spain joined the EC. For instance, before 1986, imported breakfast cereals were virtually unknown in Spain, and yet, by 1988, with little or no publicity, Weetabix was turning over £1 million. Amstrad only began selling to Spain in 1987, and within 2 years was billing over £100 million in personal computers and hi-fi equipment. Chloride Batteries set itself a £1/2 million sales target over a 4-year period and achieved the target in half the time. Further success stories abound, paying witness to the tremendous potential of the Spanish market.

Although Spain's import regulations have been relaxed significantly since EC entry, a small number of restrictions still exist. Exchange controls were abolished in February 1992. Spain's import duties have gradually been eliminated on imports from other EC countries and disappeared completely on all manufactured goods on 1 January 1993. It is necessary to present a **notificación previa** (prior notification) for certain imports and also, in some cases, an **autorización previa** (import authorization). All imports over 500,000 pesetas (in 1991) and those being financed for a period of more than 1 year must be registered with a Spanish bank and the related documentation dealt with by that bank (**domiciliación bancaria**). Imports are subject to VAT at rates of 6 per cent, 13 per cent (the most common rate) or 28 per cent, depending on their classification.

There are a number of factors exporters to Spain should bear in mind:

- *Documentation procedures.* Documentation requirements have eased considerably since Spain's accession to the EC. Advice on documentation can be obtained through banks, chambers of commerce and freight forwarders. Basically, all exports to Spain should be accompanied by the Single Administrative Document (SAD) and two sets of commercial invoices. Many products will need to meet Spanish technical standards and many food products will require special certification.
- *Customs and storage facilities.* The norm in Spain is to have rigid control of such facilities, which will be quite secure. Under certain conditions, an exporter may be able to store goods on Spanish soil for a limited period of time without incurring customs duties and may be allowed to fulfil customs-clearance requirements on his own storage premises.
- *Port of entry and domestic transport.* Inland transport within Spain is unlikely to pose any problems except in peripheral regions, since Madrid is the focal point of the road and rail network. However, it is worth verifying domestic routes before choosing the port of entry.
- *Local representation.* Although not actually required, local agents are invaluable in arranging the documentation procedures, customs

clearance and storage, and the domestic transport arrangements for imported goods. The Customs Department of the Ministry of Economy and Finance keeps a list, although it is wise to follow recommendations of the DTI or other agencies (see Researching the Spanish market, p. 121). Similarly, the engagement of an independent sales agent should follow reliable independent advice.

Joint ventures/networks

Joint ventures are proving increasingly attractive to UK companies as a means of penetrating the Spanish market using existing know-how and resources. Joint ventures appeal especially to large UK companies confident of making a significant financial commitment to the success of the venture. In Chapter 4, the experiences of major British banks such as the NatWest were described (see pp. 43–45), while Marks & Spencer has entered into a joint venture in Spain (more information below). Many other British companies have followed suit. Among them are Boots (linking with Liade), Abbey National (Grupo Cor), De La Rue (Lerchundi), BP (Petromed), Barclays (Banco de Valladolid), Mountleigh (Galerías Preciados), etc. Numerous opportunities still exist, especially in the high-tech industry, and the textile industry, which urgently needs rationalization and the application of marketing techniques from abroad.

Many Spanish businesses are indeed opting for joint ventures with counterparts in other EC countries as a means of seizing the opportunities afforded by the single market. Spain's fourth-biggest bank, the Banco de Santander, was a pioneer in this field by linking in 1989 with the Royal Bank of Scotland (see p. 44). The Banco de Santander's youthful chief executive, Juan Inciarte, typifies the new entrepreneurial breed of Spanish executive who dismisses any suggestion of Spanish inferiority, by asserting, in July 1989, 'In Spain, we have a combination of people and products second to none. That gives us a competitive advantage that foreigners cannot provide easily'.

The tie-up between the two banks justifies the Spanish bank's belief that there are other ways of growing apart from takeovers, and that flexibility is needed to cope with the wide variations between what pace 1992 are still separate and hugely different markets. The link between Banco de Santander and the Royal Bank of Scotland will bring them into each other's home markets at a fraction of the cost of building up a branch network from scratch. Juan Inciarte insists that the move towards a single financial services market is not going to happen overnight, adding that 'Many corporate institutions are looking at Europe as a single country, but if a bank does not have the ability to differentiate Scotland from Italy, it will lose in the battle for the future'. The most profitable area for collaboration looks like being between Banco de Santander's merchant bank and the Royal Bank's subsidiary, Charterhouse. The Spanish bank is keen to import expertise in financial engineering into a country where techniques such as leveraged buyouts are still in their infancy.

Spain's textile industry is another example of an industry that is now starting to look at joint ventures with foreign firms to gain access to new markets. With 315,000 legal workers and tens of thousands of undeclared ones, the textile industry is a major employer and the pillar of the economy of Catalonia. Better equipped and capitalized than ever before after a state-aided investment blitz during 1982–6, productivity has increased by 40 per cent since 1982. The recent slump in European textiles and clothing generally, plus undercutting by cheap imports, however, put the industry into deficit in 1987 and 1988. Spain's textile industry, with low wages and high levels of skill and design, but with poor marketing abroad hitherto, exemplifies the kind of business that ought to excel in the single-market context. An appreciation of the problems and the application of new marketing techniques should place this industry in an excellent position to expand during the 1990s.

The Spanish IT industry is the fastest growing in the world, at 1.5 per cent GDP in 1988, and 23 per cent growth in 1989. Predictions were that the industry would grow at four times the rate of the economy in the early and mid-1990s, but of the 1988 sales of 758,439 million pesetas only 11 per cent were accounted for by exports, suggesting again that potential for growth overseas is enormous. The Single Market represents an outstanding opportunity for IT, textiles, the banks and many other business sectors to implant themselves firmly in foreign markets. Early indications are that the Spanish business community is gearing itself up to do exactly that.

Opportunities may also be found by foreign companies in forging networking arrangements across Europe that include Spanish firms. A fee-sharing network of banks has now been formed, one combining the Hambros group in the UK with Banco Bilbao Vizcaya (BBV) in Spain and with banks in Germany and Italy. Similarly, a supermarket network has been set up, under the name Associated Marketing Services, by Argyll Foods from the UK, which owns Safeway, Presto and Lo Cost, and includes the Mercadona group in Spain. The network controls sales of £27 billion a year in 11,500 stores spread across seven countries. Inevitably, the Single Market is bound to generate further network prospects.

Joint ventures and the example of Marks & Spencer

In early 1990, Marks & Spencer embarked upon a joint venture with Cortefiel in Madrid. Marks & Spencer España is 67 per cent owned by

Table 12.2   *Specialist clothing stores*

Name	Sales turnover in 1988 (billion pesetas)	Employees	Stores
Cortefiel	28.0	2,500	70
Zara	44.0	–	95
C&A	6.0	450	6

Source: Consumer Spain '91

Marks & Spencer and 33 per cent by Cortefiel. There are plans for ten more stores across Spain to complement the first store opened in Madrid. Cortefiel is a family-owned group of department stores selling clothes. It is much smaller than El Corte Inglés and Preciados, but its importance in the clothes market is best gauged by comparing Cortefiel with other specialist clothes stores (see Table 12.2).

Cortefiel, which holds interests in several clothing manufacturers, has entered into the joint venture with Marks & Spencer in order to expand the operations of both companies in Spain. Marks & Spencer can bring to the partnership the experience of selling in Spain, which the UK company acquired through a franchising arrangement with Galerías Preciados in its Madrid and Barcelona stores. This arrangement ended in December 1991, after Marks & Spencer had generated yearly sales of 80 million pesetas through franchises. Interestingly, Mothercare is currently engaged in a similar franchising agreement with Preciados in about thirty stores.

Marks & Spencer adopts its own individual approach to retailing abroad. The company believes in taking time to become established in a new country and maintains a low profile in the marketing world, with no marketing department. Marks & Spencer first opened a store abroad in 1975, the Paris store on the Boulevard Haussmann, and now has 600 stores in nine countries, with an export business in twenty others. The St Michael brand name, classic British clothing and other goods constitute the flagship of their consumer appeal. Marks & Spencer has always been concerned to convey the same corporate message in a common corporate style in all the countries where it operates. This concern manifests itself both in the products sold and the promotional materials used by the company to market itself overseas. Wherever possible, Marks & Spencer uses products and promotional material generated in the UK as a starting point and applies a local 'stamp' to these if necessary.

One of the most interesting aspects of this joint venture is the contrast that emerges between the Spanish consumers' expectation of how a retailer operates and Marks & Spencer's attempt to export a British approach to retailing. The wider range of products as well as the distinctive nature of some of the British items on sale have clearly appealed to many Spanish customers. Although there may be problems in convincing Spanish consumers to buy gooseberry crumble, for example, the advantages of being able to buy ready-made sets of sheets or curtains, instead of the more usual Spanish practice of choosing material and having this made up, are immediately apparent. The need to educate the Spanish customer to exercise a free choice when examining products rather than expecting the traditional personal attention of a shop assistant is, however, a problem for any British retailer wishing to export home-made customs to Spain.

Education of the workforce to fit in with Marks & Spencer's corporate identity and employment traditions will also be a key factor in the company's future in Spain. Whether Marks & Spencer can repeat its French success story will be fascinating to watch, in a market where the main competitor, Zara, the leading textile group in Spain, is pioneering modern marketing methods introduced by Harvard-trained management.

Acquisitions and the example of Guinness

A prospective UK investor should obviously learn at the outset as much as possible about the business in which he is interested and should therefore employ legal and tax advisers from the beginning. Important considerations for the potential acquirer of a Spanish firm would include all the usual factors relating to the company's history, trading results and markets, but might perhaps pay special attention to an evaluation of the current management, in terms of training and linguistic ability in the investor's language, and also to a workforce evaluation, with particular attention paid to terms of employment, often more inflexible in Spain than in the UK. The location and the premises of the Spanish firm will also be a crucial element, given the regional basis of much of Spanish industry and commerce, a factor illustrated in the Guinness acquisition of La Cruz del Campo.

La Cruz del Campo SA, a well-established family brewing firm from the south, was taken over by Guinness in late 1990. It has become obvious since that date that the underlying philosophy behind Guinness's penetration of the Spanish market is to allow the Spanish company to continue to employ local knowledge and expertise.

The Spanish brewing industry dates back to the 1500s, when the King of Spain was Emperor Charles V, born in Ghent in Belgium. Although wine has traditionally been the chosen drink of Spaniards, recent years have nonetheless seen rapid growth in the consumption of beer, at the

Table 12.3 *Major brewing groups (1990)*

Name	Ownership/part ownership	% market share
La Cruz del Campo	Guinness	21.6
El Aguila	Heineken (Holland)	17.7
Damm	Oetker/Henninger (Germany)	16.9
Mahou	Kronenbourg (France)	16.1
San Miguel	San Miguel (Philippines)	13.9
Unión Cervecera	Carlsberg (Denmark)	6.5
All six major brewers		92.7
Others		7.3
		100.0

Source: El País

cost of wine. In acquiring La Cruz del Campo, Guinness has bought into a highly competitive market in which six major brewing groups, all dominated by foreign interests, control over 90 per cent of sales (see Table 12.3).

Guinness's interest in buying into an expanding Spanish market, worth almost 300 billion pesetas in 1990, is also consistent with a recent internationalization policy that has seen a Guinness link-up with LVMH, the Paris-based group that makes Moët et Chandon and Dom Pérignon champagnes, and Hennessy cognac. The Cruz del Campo acquisition may also assist Guinness's drive to promote sales in Spain of Johnnie Walker and Bell's whiskies, as well as Gordon's and Booth's gins. With light taxes on spirits in Spain, whisky sales in particular have been accelerating in recent years.

The food, drink and tobacco industry in Spain is generally ripe for foreign intervention. The industry contains mostly small companies but is one of the most important manufacturing sectors, with almost 400,000 employees. About a quarter of Spain's largest 200 companies are to be found in this sector, which has seen strong penetration by foreign multinationals. The bread market, for instance, is dominated by Bimbo (owned by Annhauser Busch, the US drinks firm) and Panrico (owned by Allied Lyons from the UK). Similarly, the meat industry is controlled by Unilever, Nestlé and Oscar Mayer from Germany.

Opportunities for UK and foreign companies rest precisely in the failings and limitations of many Spanish firms in this industry. Their lack of experience of international markets has meant little export success. Failure to invest sufficiently in product research and development has often led to a poor quality product with a poor image. If one combines this with poor distribution networks and lower levels of training among the workforce than in other EC countries, it is easy to see the attraction of linking with a stronger European neighbour.

The challenges for La Cruz del Campo as it faces up to a future within the Guinness organization is to transform its philosophy from that of a leading regional company to that of a post-1992 international company with a Spanish arm. This challenge has implications for management structures within La Cruz del Campo. The company at least has a background in marketing, unlike many Spanish firms, where the challenge is to introduce new managers trained in modern management techniques, or to acquire such skills by liaising with a foreign company. Many Spanish companies have hitherto failed to put into place a marketing management team or responsive financial reporting, or paid attention to corporate identity.

Company image and corporate identity have not been high on the list of priorities of Spanish companies generally. Moreover, financial practices of Spanish firms are bound to change – and are changing – as a result of link-ups with foreign firms or as a consequence of the need to compete efficiently. The main thrust of these changes is the need for more reliable and more regular financial monitoring and reporting. This will become more and more important as taxation changes, especially **impuestos sobre sociedades** (corporate tax), accrue from greater internationalization.

Obtaining finance

As in the UK, the Spanish private banks are the major source of short- and long-term financing for industry. They generally do not specialize, each normally being prepared to offer most of the usual banking services. They are grouped into 'industrial' and 'commercial' banks. Most of the principal banks are commercial banks but they may have industrial bank affiliates. Industrial banks specialize in providing medium- and long-term financing to new and growth companies.

Commercial banks generally provide loans for periods ranging from 3 to 6 months, which are usually renewable. It is common business practice to discount unaccepted drafts with commercial banks and in this way obtain more or less permanent bank financing. The savings banks also operate this practice and provide much of the finance for blue-chip companies and for private housing purchases.

Apart from the central bank, the Banco de España, the new state megabank, Argentaria, groups together four public banks under the control of the Ministry of Economy and Finance. They provide loans at favourable rates of interest, and are the following:

1 Banco Hipotecario de España: finances public works, construction, housing, shipbuilding, educational facilities, and lends businesses up to 70 per cent of the cost of investment projects.
2 Banco de Crédito Industrial: lends to growth industries and grants loans for working capital.
3 Banco de Crédito Agrícola: lends to farmers and agricultural co-operatives.
4 Banco de Crédito Local: finances local authorities, public transport and water supply systems.

Understanding the financial environment

In order to obtain the best financial advice possible it is essential to understand how financial backing is obtained and how payment terms are negotiated between companies and clients. Throughout Spain businesses, large and small, as well as private individuals, rely very heavily on a local agent or 'fixer', known as a **gestor**, who can conduct business with government departments and both advise on and complete paperwork on behalf of a client. Thus the **gestoría**, (agent's office) is a focal point for financial and also legal advice. For instance, a **código de identificación fiscal** (tax code) is necessary for any **contribuyente** (tax-payer), whether individual or corporate, before **pedidos** (orders) and **facturas** (invoices) can be processed. Methods of payment in Spain also do not traditionally include **talones** or cheques (cheques), which do not carry the security they do in other countries. The most usual method of payment between businesses is a **pago mediante letra (de cambio)** (bill of exchange), especially where payment is by **pagos aplazados** (instalments). Obviously, with smaller sums **pago al contado** (cash payment) is possible. With bills of exchange there is usually a 90-day, 60-day or 30-day agreement between the **fecha de factura** (date of invoice) and the **fecha de entrega** (date of delivery).

The *gestor* can also assist in obtaining financial backing for the company and in obtaining information about the creditworthiness of a potential client or partner. Any foreign company seeking to establish itself in the Spanish market must similarly be able to present full information and documentation to satisfy both trading partners and the financial institutions.

Conclusion

As the impact of the Single Market gathers pace in Spain, the opportunities for penetrating the business culture are certain to become even greater than in the period since Spain joined the EC in 1986. Whether through direct exporting, joint ventures, networks, acquisitions, or setting up a company in Spain (see pp. 32–35) the prospect of investing in Spain's future growth is a readily available one. This was not always the case in the past, but the easy accessibility of information on Spanish markets and the practical assistance offered by the DTI, chambers of commerce, the EC, etc., have made it possible for British investors to turn potential into profit. An accompanying realization of the regional dimension (see following chapter) is the final *sine qua non* of successful penetration of the Spanish business culture.

13 Penetrating the Spanish business culture II – the regional dimension

Introduction

In Chapter 1 the structure of regional government and the relationship between the seventeen autonomous regions and central government were explained (see pp. 7–9). Although there are clear differences in prosperity between the regions, these differences have more or less remained the same since the mid-1980s.

Over the period 1986–90, GDP in Spain as a whole grew by 25.5 per cent, closing the gap on the EC average; Spain in 1990 stood at 74.7 per cent of GDP per EC inhabitant, compared with 71.8 per cent in 1985. Growth in the regions was not too unequal in this period. The most expansive regions, with annual cumulative growth of more than 5 per cent, were:

- Murcia   5.4 per cent.
- Navarre   5.1 per cent.
- Valencia   5.1 per cent.
- Andalusia   5 per cent.
- Catalonia   5 per cent.

These five regions, in other words, were regions within the Mediterranean arc or on the Ebro Valley. Regions that sustained an annual growth below 4.5 per cent per cent from 1986 to 1990 were:

- Basque Country 4.4 per cent.
- Cantabria   4.3 per cent.
- Madrid   4.2 per cent.
- Castile–León   4.2 per cent.
- Galicia   4.1 per cent.

- Extremadura   3.9 per cent.
- Asturias   3.6 per cent.

This second group of seven regions was concentrated on the Cantabrian coast, the arid interior and the centre, Madrid. The five remaining regions grew annually at a rate between 4.5 per cent and 5 per cent. These regions were:

- Canaries   4.8 per cent.
- La Rioja   4.8 per cent.
- Balearics   4.7 per cent.
- Aragón   4.6 per cent.
- Castile–La Mancha 4.6 per cent.

Obviously, not all regions were starting from the same position. Madrid and Catalonia had formed the vanguard for the previous decade, while poorer regions, such as Extremadura and Galicia, were a considerable way behind development levels elsewhere in Spain. In addition, the Canaries and the Balearics were affected by a temporary 'blip' in tourism in 1989 and 1990.

However, in terms of GDP per capita, at the start of the 1990s, the north-east triangle of Spain was the most prosperous area, followed by Madrid and the Balearics: this total area comprised 49 per cent of the national population and contributed 60 per cent of GDP. At the other end of the scale, the most depressed area is the south-east, with 25 per cent of the population contributing 18 per cent of national GDP. Only the Balearics has a GDP per capita rate higher than the EC average, although Madrid and Catalonia are very close. There are four regions below two-thirds of the EC GDP per capita average: Galicia, Castile–La Mancha, Andalusia and Extremadura.

The distribution of foreign investment in Spain by region also illustrates the predominance of Madrid and Catalonia. It is shown in Table 13.1.

Madrid and Catalonia therefore accounted for almost 70 per cent of foreign investment in Spain in 1992. This represented, nonetheless, a fall on their 1991 position, when the two regions accounted for 82 per cent of foreign investment. Although it is dangerous to take one year's figures in isolation, perhaps the 1992 position suggests that foreign investors are beginning to look at other regions of the country.

Regional profiles

The advice given in the last chapter on penetrating the Spanish business market needs to be taken in conjunction with an appreciation of the

Table 13.1 *Distribution of foreign investment by region (1992)*

Region	Millions pesetas	%
Madrid	768,744.8	40.15
Catalonia	553,247.9	28.90
Valencia	166,240.1	8.68
Andalusia	100,744.0	5.26
Basque country	83,533.6	4.36
Galicia	42,226.8	2.21
Navarre	35,644.5	1.86
Balearics	27,896.4	1.46
Castile–León	19,503.7	1.02
Canaries	17,629.2	0.92
Aragón	15,581.5	0.81
Cantabria	13,873.6	0.72
Castile–La Mancha	10,654.0	0.56
Murcia	10,541.9	0.55
Asturias	5,997.9	0.31
La Rioja	5,334.7	0.28
Extremadura	1,316.2	0.07
Others	35,783.5	1.87
Total	1,914,484.3	100.00

Source: Secretaría de Estado de Comercio

trend towards taking major business decisions at regional level. In recent years, the Spanish regions have, almost without exception, taken great strides and committed large resources in attracting inward investment. Many foreign companies that have established a region presence in Spain report on the considerable practical assistance provided by the regions, not least of which is financial incentives (see previous chapter). Finding out information about the regions is, however, very difficult for a non-Spanish speaker and the regional profiles that follow concentrate on the nine (judged) most promising regions for potential trade and investment.

Catalonia (Cataluña)

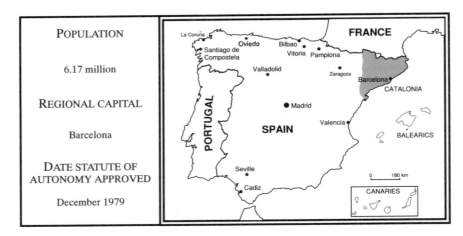

POPULATION	
6.17 million	
REGIONAL CAPITAL	
Barcelona	
DATE STATUTE OF AUTONOMY APPROVED	
December 1979	

Catalonia, situated in the north-east of Spain, bordering the south of France, is the Spanish region most likely to reap great benefits from a more united Europe. It is one of the largest and most industrially developed regions in all Spain, and within the EC only four regions have greater weight in the industrial sector: Lombardy, Stuttgart, Hamburg and Upper Franconia. The cornerstone of the Catalan economy is a well-developed industry, since Catalonia, unlike other Spanish regions, experienced its industrial revolution at the same time as other industrialized regions of Europe. Catalonia accounts for 22 per cent of Spanish exports, the highest volume per region, and 28 per cent of imports. Linked closer to Europe culturally, psychologically and economically, Catalonia absorbs about one-third of all foreign investment in Spain and is responsible for more than 40 per cent of all Spanish investment abroad. The EC accounts for 60 per cent of Catalonia's foreign trade.

Major international companies such as Volkswagen, Hewlett-Packard and Dow Chemicals are already established in Catalonia. The food industry has been thriving, based upon a prosperous agriculture and production of cava, a sparkling champagne-like drink. Massive high-tech investment has been led by the Japanese buying stakes in Catalan firms. The textile industry, which led the region's development in the last century, is ripe for foreign intervention and rationalization. The region's car industry has been very successful since Spain's indigenous SEAT models after a period under FIAT control, were incorporated into the Volkswagen group in 1982.

Catalonia also makes a significant contribution to the tourist industry, with 160 miles of Mediterranean beaches and a dozen top ski resorts in the Pyrenees. A major attraction is the excellent co-ordination between private industry and research work at Barcelona's three state universities.

The **Generalitat** (regional government) has also been co-operating with the town council in Barcelona and with the state holding corporation, the INI, to establish a technopolis near the three universities. The aim is to attract advanced technology projects specializing in robotics, biotechnology, new materials and electronics. A wide range of facilities and grants are given to firms that set up in the area, including free provision of premises. The 1992 Olympic Games in Barcelona and the high-speed rail link south to Madrid and north to France have inevitably generated further business activity in this, the most dynamic of Spain's regions.

Madrid

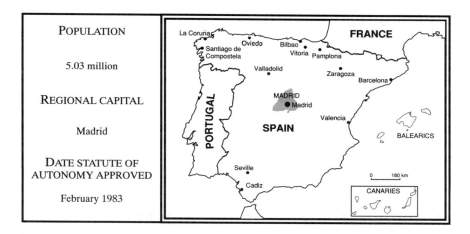

POPULATION	
5.03 million	
REGIONAL CAPITAL	
Madrid	
DATE STATUTE OF AUTONOMY APPROVED	
February 1983	

Madrid's importance as an industrial centre dates from the 1960s, as a result of development plans carried out by the Franco regime. The population swelled as Spaniards flooded in from depressed rural areas. Today, the population growth is close to zero in Madrid, but economic analysts are predicting a new upsurge in industrial activity and population with the arrival of the Single European Market.

Madrid experienced growth pains in the 1980s, attracting the highest level of direct foreign investment, much of it in technological and industrial areas. Sharply rising real estate prices, reflecting a demand from businesses with an eye on the European market, have seen a population move to the suburbs and a tremendous shortage of housing for young people. While Madrid has become one of Europe's top cities of investment, it still faces major transportation and communications problems, being perhaps the most isolated of all EC capital cities, with the highest altitude and surrounded by mountains. The high-speed rail tracks to the south and to the north have not come a day too soon for Madrid, which also needs a much more extensive radial motorway network to other parts of the country.

Madrid-based enterprises are leading the way in joint ventures with other countries. The telecommunications giant Telefónica, a combined private and state-owned monopoly, is spearheading a drastic revamping of the country's telecommunications network and is currently developing a joint European venture to produce a mobile telephone system that will be internationally compatible. Another major company set to benefit from this internationalization process is Tabacalera, originally a tobacco firm, but whose diverse products are now marketed throughout the world via joint ventures. In the UK, for instance, the company holds a 49.5 per cent stake in Eagle Star insurance and is a major partner in food production and tourist chains throughout the European community. Tabacalera is to join forces with Nabisco in the new European market after 1993.

Madrid is of course also the hub of the country's financial network. Caja de Madrid is the most profitable of Spain's savings banks and is also Spain's leading savings bank in terms of credit granted and customers' deposits (see pp. 45–46). The bank's positive attitude towards European financial integration at the end of 1992 was perhaps typical of Madrid's self-confidence as a whole. Anticipating more competition, shrinking profits and a demand for greater productivity, Spanish bankers nevertheless look forward to establishing co-operation agreements with foreign banks and the opportunity to distribute their products in other markets.

Andalusia (Andalucia)

POPULATION	
7.10 million	
REGIONAL CAPITAL	
Seville	
DATE STATUTE OF AUTONOMY APPROVED	
December 1981	

Andalusia has traditionally relied on agriculture as its main source of employment and principal earner. Much of the agricultural system has, however, been slow to invest in new farming methods. Migration to other parts of Spain or abroad has often been the chosen escape route for thousands of Andalusians, and unemployment, currently standing at 24 per cent, has always been high. There has been little industrial tradition in the region, despite massive development around Seville in the past 20 years, with 60 per cent working in the services sector, mostly in tourism. An estimated 3 million people depend indirectly on EC subsidies, and per capita GDP, at 54.5 per cent of the EC average, compares with a national average of 76.7 per cent and 99.1 per cent in the Madrid region.

The hope of the regional government was that Expo '92 in Seville would catapult the region into the twenty-first century. An enormous infrastructural build-up has already taken place, with thousands of kilometres of new roads, a new airport, railway station and opera house, in addition to the high-speed rail link with Madrid. The region's future is dependent upon a 1991–4 economic development plan, which started in October 1991 and which aims to modernize the production system; it set aside 80 billion pesetas over 4 years to assist the creation of new companies and the technological overhaul of existing ones. The plan also allocates funds for the training of future managers. Despite the plan, problems remain for the region, especially the road communications network, which provides good links between Seville and Madrid, and other important regional centres such as Córdoba and Huelva, but which is appalling in the Málaga and Almería area.

A number of multinationals pledged themselves to stay on the Expo site after 1992, and there are encouraging signs of new technological developments being sited in the region. The state-owned aerospace firm, CASA, is developing carbon-fibre avionics at its plant outside Seville. Malaga has induced Hughes Microelectronics from the UK to produce sophisticated components in its Science Park. With a prime minister in Madrid representing Seville in parliament and with the undoubted impetus of Expo, Andalusia is set to cast off its 'poor neighbour' image.

Valencia

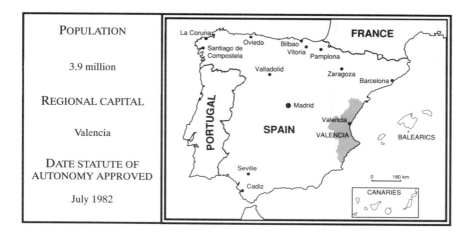

POPULATION	
3.9 million	
REGIONAL CAPITAL	
Valencia	
DATE STATUTE OF AUTONOMY APPROVED	
July 1982	

Visitors to Benidorm and beaches around Alicante may not realize that tourism is only one of three main sectors of this region's economy. The other two are industry and agriculture. Half of Europe's oranges and lemons come from this region. In addition, Spain's biggest automobile factory, near the city of Valencia, distributes Fords all over Europe. The highly successful Lladró ceramic firm is also in Valencia. Tourists, farmers and industrialists have all benefited from great improvements in the road network, which now includes bypasses around Valencia and Alicante to allow a continuous motorway route from Alicante to Perpignan in France. More upgrading of roads to dual carriageway and the prospect of a new high-speed rail link down the coast to Alicante will assist the regional growth rate, which has been well above the national average since 1987.

Several factors have contributed to Valencia's recent industrial growth, notably a boost in local investment and reinvestment, substantial expansion in the construction sector and the development of new, non-traditional industries. Industry, often with foreign investment and technological updating, has begun a massive transformation. Traditional Valencian industry consists of areas such as textiles, shoes, toys and furniture. New industries are emerging, especially industrial machinery and high-tech, to change the region's profile. Traditional industry now represents 47 per cent of the industrial sector, a drop of five points in 5 years, while new sectors account for approximately 52 per cent. The majority of new investment has, however, come from within the region. The Valencian banking sector, too, is undergoing transformation, especially the Bank of Valencia. After suffering serious economic problems involving the real estate industry, the Bank of Valencia now has multiple investments in different sectors of the region's economy and itself has hundreds of foreign investors.

Although it accounts for 16 per cent of Spain's industrial exports, Valencia still lags behind Catalonia to the north, although Valencia's trade balance is better. Attempts to improve export performance characterize many Valencian firms. One of the oldest companies, Monerris Planellis SA, maker of turrón, a nougat-style confectionery popular at Christmas, has always been strong in exports to South and North America, but has recently been in talks with UK and German firms to broaden its network. Such readiness to internationalize on the part of many Valencian companies, allied with good regional infrastructure and a healthy economy, gives this region a head start over most others in Spain.

The Basque Country (El Pais Vasco)

POPULATION	
2.16 million	
REGIONAL CAPITAL	
Vitoria	
DATE STATUTE OF AUTONOMY APPROVED	
December 1979	

The Basques have always preserved their distinctive character, founded upon a fierce pride in their own mysterious language and a tradition of separate development from the rest of Spain throughout most of their history. The heartland of Spanish heavy industry, with iron and steelworks and shipyards, the Basque country has had to contend with political extremism from the diehard terrorist group ETA, while at the same time trying to rebuild the Basque economy and foreign investment, at an all-time low after the 1973 oil crisis. Today, the region has a steadily improving modern economy with growth rates well above the European average.

Under a plan called the Special Europe '93 Plan, the Basques are currently updating their telecommunications industry. To do so, they need industrial investment, and the Basque regional government is offering generous financial inducements and credit terms to foreign investors, with the greatest levels of support destined for high-tech projects. The UK and the Basque country have a long history of economic and industrial relations, but, by 1975, British investment in the Basque Country was virtually zero. Since 1984, however, when the British Chamber of Commerce began to have some influence, a number of British companies have participated in joint ventures in the region. The Bilbao superport is one of the most important in Europe, and the anticipated creation of a central bank in the Basque Country would provide further credit for interested investors.

A new, younger generation of Basque business people, who have travelled abroad and know English, are leading local and foreign-financed firms. Alongside the newcomers, long-standing industries, such as the iron and steel giant Altos Hornos de Vizcaya, will continue to play a major role. After a rationalization and economic recovery programme in the 1980s, Altos Hornos, as Spain's leading private steel company, is well able to compete internationally. Similarly, with Babcock and Wilson Española, a well-established manufacturer of metal pipe, iron castings, machine tools and gas cylinders. The Basque country is also home to the giant co-operative group Mondragón, one of the most successful co-operatives in the world (see p. 33).

The activities of ETA have undoubtedly damaged the region's image and its industries. However, the Basque people have demonstrated their rejection of the terrorists, and the region's combination of traditional and new industries suggests a brighter future.

Castile–Leon (Castilla–Leon)

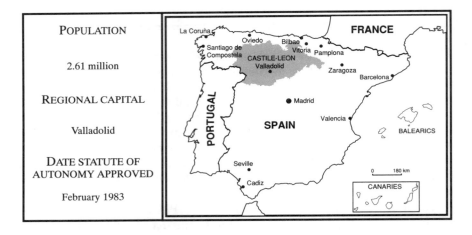

POPULATION	
2.61 million	
REGIONAL CAPITAL	
Valladolid	
DATE STATUTE OF AUTONOMY APPROVED	
February 1983	

Castile–Leon is Spain's largest region, accounting for 18 per cent of national territory, and one of the richest in natural resources. The region has large resources of uranium in Salamanca and iron in Leon, and is a leading mining region, with 25 per cent of national mineral production and 35 per cent of total mineral reserves. Food production is important, with emphasis on livestock, wheat, barley and vegetables. Tobacco and wood products are also major contributors to the economy of a region still relying on agriculture for the bulk of its wealth. Following Spain's entry into the EC, the region's sales to other countries have increased by more than 25 per cent, although Castile–Leon accounts for less than 3 per cent of the national export total and buys less than 20 per cent of the country's imports. The region's many exports include machinery and electrical equipment, metals, leather, and animal and vegetable fats and oils.

The great challenge for this region is industrial development, since much of industry is backward. To attract new investment, the regional government has provided public land for factories and warehouses, and has at its disposal a whole host of incentives to promote technological investment and job creation. The private investor is the stated priority of the region's centrist coalition government, which is committed to a policy of improving the regional infrastructure to create the right climate for investors. The region wants to improve the road and motorway links to Portugal and the Atlantic seaboard in Galicia and Asturias. There is also the possibility of a high-speed rail link through Castile–Leon, which, if it became a reality, would run from the French border either to Lisbon or Oporto in Portugal.

Currently, the region's industrial sector comprises various subsectors such as coalmining, hydraulic and thermal energy and uranium production. Tourism is relatively underdeveloped, although it has considerable potential, since Castile–Leon is rich in cultural and historical artefacts, along with its lakes, mountains and varied countryside.

Galicia

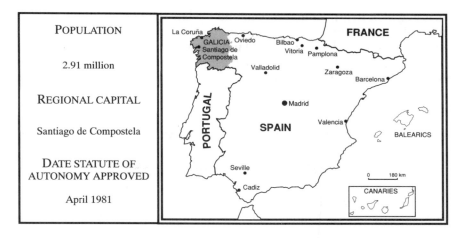

POPULATION	
2.91 million	
REGIONAL CAPITAL	
Santiago de Compostela	
DATE STATUTE OF AUTONOMY APPROVED	
April 1981	

Fishing, coupled with agriculture and livestock production, has always been the economic lifeline of Galicia. The region is strategically situated on the Atlantic, with two major port cities, Vigo and La Coruña. Galicia, with only 7 per cent of Spain's population, produces half the fish products consumed in Spain, as well as 25 per cent of the country's agriculture, 30 per cent of its forestry resources and 20 per cent of its livestock. Although firmly anchored in traditional sectors, industry is sprouting under the regional government's new industrialization and modernization plan, which aims to bring the region in line with highly industrialized regions such as Catalonia and the Basque Country. Industry has begun to take off, especially around La Coruña, but much remains to be done.

The fishing industry will inevitably continue to play a major role in the Galician economy. Vigo, one of the most important ports in Europe and top of the European league for the movement of fresh fish, plays the double role of fuelling the fish industry and stimulating commerce. Among the most important fishing companies is Pescanova, established in 1960 as a distant-water trawling company. It has pioneered various techniques in the highly competitive fishing industry, its fleet being the first in Europe to incorporate an on-board refrigeration system. It also pioneered the setting up in Spain of the first organized distribution network of deep-frozen foods covering the entire country. Investment in research, both in fishing and food technology, has paid off, giving Pescanova the leading position it occupies today as a fishing company and a frozen-food producer and distributor.

The Galician government is conscious of the region's backward image and wants to give tourism a greater role in the regional economy. Current projects and objectives include improving the quality of beaches, ocean-related sports, and hotel expansion and promotion. The Department of Industry and Trade in the region has also embarked upon a massive plan to attract investment and update the region. Stimulation of technological institutes and areas set aside for technological development, the renovation of industrial infrastructure and the encouragement of small and medium-sized companies, represent some of the initiatives being taken to ensure that Galicia is fully integrated into post-1992 Europe.

Asturias

POPULATION	
1.13 million	
REGIONAL CAPITAL	
Oviedo	
DATE STATUTE OF AUTONOMY APPROVED	
December 1981	

Asturias has been the coalmining centre of Spain since the eighteenth century and is blessed with large deposits of zinc, iron and other mineral resources. It is a mountainous and forested region, and sustains remote farming communities alongside traditional and newly established industries. In the past 15 years, significant industrial progress has been made in all areas, including agriculture, farming and mining. But the regional government is anxious to attract more foreign investment by advertising the availability of land for further development and by improving the generally good communications and transport networks.

In the run-up to 1993, the regional government offered grants of up to 45 per cent on approved investment in the region. These grants consist of soft loans, guarantees for loans, privileged credit and other incentives. The attempt to boost foreign investment has been successful, with important foreign companies now located in Asturias. These include Alcan, the Canadian aluminium-processing company; Agar de Asturias SA, a US–Mexican chemical firm; Bel Asturias, a UK milk company; and Celulosas de Asturias SA, a paper paste industry supported by British capital. The US company Dupont has invested over 1 billion dollars in an industrial chemical complex, and Siemens and Corning Glass are combining to set up Spain's first optical-fibre plant.

The Asturian government has created the Regional Development Institute, an independent agency designed to support balanced industrial development in the region while at the same time preserving the region's picturesque features, such as its mountains and beaches. Quality tourism is on the increase in a region that has provided evidence of its ability to develop new industries in the built-up triangle between the regional capital, Oviedo, and two coastal towns, Gijón and Avilés, both important ports and shipyards. Fifteen years ago, this triangle enclosed a landscape dotted with farms and villages. Now there is a patchwork of roads, industrial estates and dozens of new companies.

Navarre (Navarra)

POPULATION	
0.53 million	
REGIONAL CAPITAL	
Pamplona	
DATE STATUTE OF AUTONOMY APPROVED	
August 1982	

Navarre is the home of the city of Pamplona, known worldwide for its annual bull-running festival. Less well known is the remarkable transformation of the region from a predominantly rural economy to a highly industrialized one, all in one generation. Navarre has a per capita income above the Spanish average, while its middle class comprises an estimated 80 per cent of the population. Some eighty multinational companies, including General Electric and Volkswagen, have bases in the region, which, situated on the French border, is strategically well-located for business, with the added inducement of generous government investment. Major infrastructural projects are under way, including the construction of highways to lure European travellers into Spain via Navarre and to create smoother links to other Spanish regions. Communications and educational facilities are also being upgraded to include a new state university.

Crucial to the economic upturn of the region was the creation in the mid-1980s of SODENA, or Society for the Development of Navarre, which has acted as a conduit between local firms and prospective foreign partners. Although the region's agricultural sector is important, the industrial sector is even more powerful. It is dominated by the automobile and car parts industry, and several automobile giants are based in Navarre, notably SEAT, Volkswagen, Nissan and Motor Ibérica.

Regional companies have also stepped up investment in recent years in a bid to become more competitive and to extend international markets. The food producer Viscofan, by dint of substantial investment in research and development, has become a leader in technology applied to the food-processing and packaging industry. It has also captured new markets in Australia, Canada and Japan.

Tourism is not a major earner for Navarre, but a recent survey, showing that Navarre has been second only to Catalonia in its success at wooing foreign investment, indicates that Navarre can more than compensate industrially.

Conclusion

Penetrating the Spanish business culture is clearly dependent upon understanding how the business environment functions, and the regional dimension is a vital factor alongside the many aspects covered in previous chapters.

In the UK in 1991 there were twenty-six seminars on trading in Spain held under various auspices, in addition to trade missions from all parts of the country. The Department of Trade and Industry alone ran twenty-two presentations as part of its 'Spotlight on Spain campaign' in late 1991 and 1992. Media coverage of Spain has never been as high, and advice and assistance on penetrating the Spanish market never so readily available. It is worth, at this juncture, reiterating a number of important lessons so that interest and information can be transformed into success:

- Some knowledge of the language is desirable, especially when it must *not* be assumed that all, or even most, Spaniards can do business in English. In trade missions to Spain the language barrier has been seen as the biggest anxiety among potential venturers into the Spanish market. It is wise to have trade leaflets, brochures and other forms of promotional material available in Spanish from the outset. In the absence of language competence, local people who speak Spanish and English should be employed.
- Spanish accounting and financial systems *are* different and require a British company to engage local financial and legal advice, preferably from Spaniards who understand something of British business practice.
- Time, patience and a strong constitution *will* be necessary in dealing with what, to the British business person, may seem like needless bureaucracy or unnecessary procrastination. Paperwork may be heavy but, once in a queue, it is better to persist until the problem is solved. Letters may be ignored, and telephone calls should be used where personal contact is not possible. Spaniards will take time in forging a personal business relationship, often in social situations, and although tough negotiators, they will nonetheless remain friends.
- Although massive changes *have* taken place in the business environment in recent years, a certain insularity (a hangover from the Franco era) may be encountered in some business sectors. Prospective partners are unlikely to be hostile to foreign intervention but may be somewhat apprehensive of the implications.

Many foreign companies and business people have been successful in meeting Spanish business culture halfway. The events of 1992 in Spain provided a springboard for other foreign companies interested in the Spanish market. Britain's approach to Expo '92 was described by the UK government in these terms in 1990: 'Expo '92 in Seville will provide an important opportunity to promote the resurgence of British business, technology and services'. The year 1492 and the discovery of America heralded the beginning of Seville's – and Spain's – golden age, with the southern Spanish city the trade capital of the new world. Beyond 1993, the grandiose project of Cartuja '93 is intended to map out a high-tech future for Seville and Spain. Despite problems – an unemployment rate which is still the highest in the EC, and sporadic ETA terrorism – a spirit of innovation pervades the Spanish business scene. The opportunity is there for a new discovery, the discovery of Spain by many more members of the foreign business community.

Sources and suggestions for further reading

Anuario El País, published yearly, Madrid: Altamira.

Cambio 16, published weekly, Madrid.

Donaghy, P.J. and Newton, M.T. (1987), *Spain: A Guide to Political and Economic Institutions*, Cambridge: CUP.

Economist, Surveys on Spain.

El País, published daily, Madrid.

Euromonitor, Book of European Regions 1992.

European Business Conspectus.

European Marketing Data and Statistics 1992.

European Commission Statistics.

European Commission, *Panorama of EC Industries 1991/2*.

European Information Development (1983), *Problems of Enlargement. Taking Stock and Proposals*, London.

Financial Times, Conference 19–20 November 1990, Madrid – *Business with Spain: Strategies for Developing Competitiveness*. Conference 20–21 November 1991, Madrid – *Spain's Role in the New Europe*.

Gillespie, R. (1989), *The Spanish Socialist Party*, Oxford: Clarendon Press.

Gilmour, D. (1985), *The Transformation of Spain*, London: Quartet.

Graham, R. (1984), *Spain. Change of a Nation*, London: Michael Joseph.

Harrison, J. (1978), *An Economic History of Modern Spain*, Manchester University Press.

Hooper, J. (1986), *The Spaniards*, London: Penguin.

Mercado, Anuario, published yearly, Madrid: Lerner.

OECD Economic Surveys, Spain, Paris, 1989.

OECD Statistics, OECD Publications, Paris.

Preston, P. (1986), *The Triumph of Democracy in Spain*, London: Methuen.

Preston, P. and Smith, D. (1984), *Spain, the EEC and NATO*, London: RKP.

Randlesome, C. *et al.* (1993), *Business Cultures in Europe*, Oxford: Butterworth-Heinemann.

Readers' Digest, Eurodata 1990.

Sagardoy Bengoechea, J.A. and León Blanco, D. (1982), *El Poder Sindical en España*, Barcelona: Planeta.

Salmon, K. (1991), *The Modern Spanish Economy*, London: Pinter Publishers.

Sampedro, J.L. and Payno, M.A. (1983), *The Enlargement of the European Community – Case Studies of Greece, Portugal and Spain*, London: Macmillan.

Shlaim, A. and Yannopoulous, G.N. (eds) (1976), *The EEC and the Mediterranean Countries*, Cambridge: CUP.

Index